Textiles on Film

Textiles on Film

Becky Peterson

BLOOMSBURY VISUAL ARTS
LONDON • NEW YORK • OXFORD • NEW DELHI • SYDNEY

BLOOMSBURY VISUAL ARTS
Bloomsbury Publishing Plc, 50 Bedford Square, London, WC1B 3DP, UK
Bloomsbury Publishing Inc, 1359 Broadway, New York, NY 10018, USA
Bloomsbury Publishing Ireland, 29 Earlsfort Terrace, Dublin 2, D02 AY28, Ireland

BLOOMSBURY, BLOOMSBURY VISUAL ARTS and the Diana logo are trademarks of Bloomsbury Publishing Plc

First published in Great Britain 2024
Paperback edition published 2025

Copyright © Becky Peterson, 2024

Becky Peterson has asserted her right under the Copyright, Designs and Patents Act, 1988, to be identified as Author of this work.

For legal purposes the Acknowledgments on p. xiv constitute an extension of this copyright page.

Cover design by Adriana Brioso
Cover image: The brothers Louis and Auguste Lumière, inventors of color photography and creators of one of the earliest film cameras.
(© Apic/Getty Images)

All rights reserved. No part of this publication may be: i) reproduced or transmitted in any form, electronic or mechanical, including photocopying, recording or by means of any information storage or retrieval system without prior permission in writing from the publishers; or ii) used or reproduced in any way for the training, development or operation of artificial intelligence (AI) technologies, including generative AI technologies. The rights holders expressly reserve this publication from the text and data mining exception as per Article 4(3) of the Digital Single Market Directive (EU) 2019/790.

Bloomsbury Publishing Plc does not have any control over, or responsibility for, any third-party websites referred to or in this book. All internet addresses given in this book were correct at the time of going to press. The author and publisher regret any inconvenience caused if addresses have changed or sites have ceased to exist, but can accept no responsibility for any such changes.

A catalogue record for this book is available from the British Library.

A catalog record for this book is available from the Library of Congress.

ISBN: HB: 978-1-3500-2655-1
PB: 978-1-3504-3072-3
ePDF: 978-1-3500-2656-8
eBook: 978-1-3500-2657-5

Typeset by Deanta Global Publishing Services, Chennai, India

For product safety related questions contact productsafety@bloomsbury.com.

To find out more about our authors and books visit www.bloomsbury.com and sign up for our newsletters.

For Brian and Henry

Contents

List of Illustrations	viii
Preface	x
Acknowledgments	xiv
Introduction: Converging Technologies: Fabric and Film	1
1 Modern Women Wear Satin: Fabric, Femininity, and Art Deco Hollywood	19
2 "That Polyester Look": Cinematic/Synthetic/Aesthetic	43
3 Screen Prints: Striping and Cinematic Language	65
4 Watching Is Touching: On-Screen Transgressions	91
5 Moving Pictures: Magic, Suspense, and Textiles in Motion	111
Conclusion: Digital Experimentation and the Legacy of the Handmade	131
Notes	139
Bibliography	169
Filmography	179
Index	181

Illustrations

0.1	Moving material through a sewing machine	2
1.1	Fred Astaire and Ginger Rogers dancing in *Top Hat*	24
1.2	Fred Astaire dancing in *Top Hat*	26
1.3	Louise Brooks as Lulu, wearing white satin on the set of *Pandora's Box*	30
1.4	Louise Brooks as Lulu	31
1.5	Louise Brooks as Lulu, confronting Schön (Fritz Kortner)	32
1.6	Promotional poster for *Flying Down to Rio*	36
1.7	Robot Maria (Brigitte Helm)'s face as she incites chaos among male viewers with her provocative dancing	39
2.1	John Travolta and Karen Lynn Gorney in *Saturday Night Fever*	50
2.2	Divine as Francine Fishpaw	55
2.3	Promotional poster for *Jeanne Dielman, 23, quai du commerce, 1080 Bruxelles*	62
3.1	Promotional poster for *Black Girl*	72
3.2	Mbissine Thérèse Diop as Diouana	74
3.3	Mbissine Thérèse Diop as Diouana	75
3.4	Theda Bara as a vamp in *A Fool There Was*	77
3.5	Brad Davis in *Querelle*	81
3.6	Joan Crawford and Ann Blyth in *Mildred Pierce*	84
3.7	Zachary Scott and Ann Blyth in *Mildred Pierce*	85
3.8	Zachary Scott, Ann Blyth, and Joan Crawford in Mildred's office. *Mildred Pierce*	86
3.9	Eve Arden as Ida and Joan Crawford as Mildred, in Mildred's office	88

4.1	Kyle MacLachlan and Isabella Rossellini (wearing a blue velvet robe) in *Blue Velvet*	98
4.2	Claudette Colbert and Clark Gable in *It Happened One Night*	108
5.1	Cyd Charisse and Gene Kelly in *Singin' in the Rain*	113
5.2	Two nuns commiserating in the palace	119
5.3	David Farrar, as Mr. Dean, his exposed skin contrasting with the nuns' heavy garments, in *Black Narcissus*	120
5.4	Judith Anderson as Mrs. Danvers	122
5.5	Josette Day as Belle, wearing gifts from the Beast in *La Belle et la Bête*	126
5.6	Josette Day as Belle in *La Belle et la Bête*	128

Preface

"Poetry from the Future"

Peau d'âne (*Donkey Skin*), the 1970 film directed by Jacques Demy based on a Charles Perrault fairy tale, includes a prop that, for me, embodies the poetic work of cross-disciplinary thinking. The prop—a dress "the color of the weather"—intriguingly combines fabric with projected imagery. Re-watching *Peau d'âne*, I see the film as a richly colored, emotionally heightened illustration of the creative process and the work of research. My interest in textiles and film emerged out of studying poetry and poetics, and I have continued to see the joint investigation of textiles and film as a sort of poetic metaphor: textiles are films; films are textiles.

In an early scene in the film, the king, a widower who promised his now-dead wife that he would marry again only if he finds a woman as beautiful as she, decides his own daughter is the one person who can fill this role. In his attempt to seduce the princess, he reads poetry to her. He selects from books featuring "poetry from the future," noting that he believes she would prefer "the poets of tomorrow" to ancient poets. After he proposes marriage, his daughter blames the poems, saying they are "troubling" and that the poetry "deranges" him. For help, the princess turns to her godmother—who gave the books of poems to the king and who orchestrates much of the film's narrative movement—and they decide she should put her father off by asking for a series of gifts before agreeing to marriage. The gifts are dresses made from cloth of "impossible" colors: one the color of the sun, one the color of the moon, and one the color of the weather.

The scene, a day later, in which we are shown the princess's new "weather"-colored dress, presents us with a memorable image of textiles and film merged on screen. A group of seamstresses carry the heavy garment (said to be made of actual film screen material) to the princess. She puts it on behind a privacy screen and emerges wearing the magical, "impossible" dress. A film of clouds moving continuously across a blue sky is projected on the fabric of the dress. Like a film screen hanging on a wall, the projected image transforms material into a dynamic, multidimensional textile—the fabric becomes film.

The dress itself is, in addition to its "impossibility," not a practical, everyday garment. Its weight makes it clearly difficult for the princess to manage. The dress acts like a piece of art—a kind of cinematic "poetry from the future"—rather than a typical body covering. The presence of textiles on the film screen, too, marks a change in the textile's use. Detached from practical, physical, and other real-life concerns, textiles on film are in the realm of art. This reframing is foundational to my study, which considers textiles as they are used in the particular, projected worlds of filmmaking and film-watching.

The "weather"-colored dress touches on several themes I investigate in this book. The dress works as a visual metaphor, showing at once how a textile can act like a film and how a film can take on the qualities of a textile. I have found the work of unraveling and articulating these shifting lines among media to be challenging and productive. As artist Sabrina Gschwandtner writes: "When I'm asked what I do I often reply that I'm an artist who works with film, video and textiles. To me the link between the three is instinctive and implicit—media is a textile—and my work expresses why and how I find that to be true."[1]

The representation of motion, the inclusion of the fantastic alongside the realistic, and the focus on an impossible object of desire—the body of the princess as well as the dress itself—are captured within this screen/dress. A nonverbal image, the dress translates the metaphorical aspect of poetry into cinematic form.

My interest in textiles began with poetry. Poetry has taught me much about reading closely, and it is the practice of close-reading literature combined with a more broad study of several disciplines that compelled me to investigate interconnected questions about language, material, and visual art. Trying to straddle the world of the tangible (fabric) and the world of the intangible (film) through language is similar to the act of reading or writing poetry, and writing a book about textiles and film has felt like a return to exploring the relationship between material objects and the written word. Working with different forms and materials while attempting to define their connections and limits can be a creative approach to academic scholarship, as is work across disciplines. Thinking about textiles with films-as-texts, while building my historical and theoretical knowledge, has been eye-opening and humbling.

As an MFA student in creative writing, I discovered the work of Laura Riding Jackson. Struck by her theoretical rigor and creative talent, I began to study her poetry, essays, and biography—this set me on a path toward serious study of dress, textiles, and ornamentation. At the same time as she was accepted by a conservative, largely male poetry establishment, Riding Jackson wrote about the highly feminized, trivialized topics of jewelry and clothing. In addition, Riding Jackson was born into a family with roots in the garment industry and factory labor.

In my doctoral program, I continued pursuing my research into Riding Jackson, and eventually expanded my scholarship to include the work of other twentieth-century women artists who wrote creatively and theoretically about dress and ornamentation. I identified with the concerns of these women artists, who felt compelled to devote serious study to what is often perceived as not serious. Filmmaker Maya Deren, weaver Anni Albers, and poets Gertrude Stein, Mina Loy, and Lorine Niedecker all wrote about textiles and clothing in addition to incorporating these objects into their art. In conjunction with my literary studies I read and studied the disciplines of dress, textile, and craft studies, and eventually incorporated film, another art form, into my project.

My family lineage of anonymous workers and forgotten textile laborers was an important force driving my initial examination of factory work and unionization in the early 20th century. My academic experience working in the precarious positions of graduate student instructor and then adjunct faculty member, as well as in the domestic struggle of parental work, further complicated how I viewed the interconnected worlds of industry and craft, factory and home-based labor.

The study of textiles has provided me with a point of entry for delving into these issues, and has unearthed a wealth of interdependent questions about the impact of textiles on cinema, the effect of film on fabrics, the tension between the verbal and nonverbal, and the impact of historical and cultural movements on media. Initially provoked by fascinating and "troubling" poems, I have found myself exploring this unlikely thing: the multifaceted world of screens and dresses, films and textiles.

Acknowledgments

I have been fortunate to be surrounded by nurturing, thoughtful writers, thinkers, and teachers in the places where I have lived, studied, and worked. Many kind friends, family members, and colleagues have made this book possible.

When I began graduate study, as an MFA student at Mills College, I was introduced to books and scholars who continue to inspire me. As a doctoral student in the University of Minnesota Department of English, I found encouragement and intellectual inspiration as I began researching and investigating the interdisciplinary ideas I explore in this study. I am grateful to the University of New Mexico Feminist Research Institute, which provided me with a scholar-in-residence position while writing this book. The team at Bloomsbury has offered crucial assistance and advice since the beginning of this project; I am grateful to them and to the manuscript readers, who all provided valuable feedback.

I am particularly indebted to my husband, Brian DiDonna, and our son, Henry DiDonna, for their love and support. Special thanks is owed to my father, Richard B. Peterson, who has always encouraged my writing.

Introduction

Converging Technologies: Fabric and Film

Dziga Vertov's 1929 silent film *Man with a Movie Camera* includes scenes in which the worlds of textile-making and filmmaking collide on screen. The juxtaposition of images, a central technique in Vertov's circle, creates a productive "collision" of ideas. A technically innovative record of Soviet urban daily life, *Man with a Movie Camera* repeatedly references itself as a made object; for example, the camera often pulls back to show us the filmmaker at work. Making films is placed in conjunction with other types of work: Vertov pays close, critical attention to the mechanics of multiple industries and to the way workers interact with industrialized machinery. Vertov's cinematic conflation of textile production and film production articulates my aim with this study: to draw from the specific languages of both film and textile studies in order to provoke questions about culture and materiality.

Vertov encourages us to link the making of textiles and films several times, particularly in correlating the wheel-based motion of trains, cameras, and industrialized thread/sewing machines.[1] The (largely female) workforce behind the sewing/textile and the film editing industries is given special attention. An especially evocative example occurs mid-way through the film, in a sequence that connects the acts of threading and sewing with the work of winding the film camera and cutting film strips. Transitioning from images of a woman getting a manicure, the film turns its focus to the hands and fingertips of women workers manipulating fabric and celluloid. Vertov prompts us to consider parallels in the physical experiences of sewing and film editing, and specifically in the relationship of the human hand to the machine. We move back and forth between close-ups of fabric moving through a sewing machine and celluloid moving over a light box.

In this approximately one-minute-long sequence, Vertov includes images that argue for a cross-disciplinary appreciation of materials and usage: scissors as implements for cutting hair, fabric, and film strips; pedals and wheels as crucial equipment in sewing and editing; levers and lenses as extensions of human bodies. In bringing together the fields of textile studies and film studies, I build on the ideas sparked by this brief but significant moment in *Man with a Movie Camera*. Using a montage editing technique that cross-cuts between images, Vertov creates layered connections and visual resonances. Interdisciplinary

Figure 0.1 Moving material through a sewing machine. Credit: *Man with a Movie Camera* (dir. Dziga Vertov, 1929), British Film Institute Video.

scholarship has provided me with a similar experience: the juxtaposition of textile studies and film studies has been particularly fruitful in introducing concepts into both fields of scholarship.

Why put textiles and films in conversation? What happens when we look closely at the role fabrics play on screen? Textiles and films emerged from overlapping historical, material, and technological conditions. Films use textiles to signify and suggest meaning. Thinking about fabrics, with their inherent connection to touch and texture, alongside the two-dimensional film screen, highlights unnoticed aspects of both types of media. The presence of textiles on screen means that they are mediated through the mechanisms—lens, position, projection—of the film camera. How might technological advances and limitations impact how we "read" and communicate through textiles?

Factory-based textile production, in the eighteenth and nineteenth centuries, saw an increasing reliance on mass production and innovation in the widespread distribution of products; a century later, the rise of film technology and the developing film industry experienced a similar dependence on large numbers of workers. While the rapid growth of the film and textile industries made cinema and fiber-based goods more globally accessible—as Rebecca Solnit writes, "photographic reproduction would make the world's images and experiences as available as the Manchester mills made cotton fabric"—large-scale production and distribution required masses of workers.[2] The labor of many underpaid, unrecognized people across the world was and continues to be foundational to both of these industries. Parallel histories of technological advances and exploitative factory labor practices intersect and problematize the two fields. While the histories of the textile and film industries are not identical, taking their simultaneous development into account has helped me to contextualize the role of fabric in the specific films I discuss.

To explain the mechanics of piecing together film material, film editors have relied on the physical similarities between sewing and editing.³ The similar operations of sewing machines and film cameras—pulling material through sprockets; the intermittent movement of camera shutters and needles—have long connected makers in these two disciplines. Filmmaker Mary Lance recalls:

> I remember having a problem threading a Moviola flatbed, an editing table, when I was starting to work with 16mm film in the late 1970s. That type had torque motors that could snap and break the film if they weren't threaded properly. I flashed on threading a sewing machine when I was much younger and realized that that process had been confusing at first, then became second nature. Threading Moviolas soon became routine too.⁴

Walter Murch's book *In the Blink of an Eye*, often used in classes on film editing, describes the process of editing celluloid strips as a reworking of the scene so that "the shots themselves seem to create each other: this shot 'makes' the next shot, which 'makes' the next shot, etc."⁵ The work of editing, for Murch, is a process of building and joining, not unlike the work of sewing, quilting, and other fiber arts.

In photographs from the early twentieth century, film editing rooms look remarkably similar to rooms in textile and clothing factories: lines of desks or tables with bent-over women threading material through large machinery. It was the association of film editing with sewing that led editing departments to hire women for the job. Erin Hill describes how women were always part of filmmaking, though they were usually relegated to "insignificant, tedious, low status, and noncreative" labor.⁶ Women in editing departments "assembled" and "patched" the film strips. As in textile production and factory work, women making films were (and often still are) anonymous and uncredited. Hill writes that in costuming as well as in editing, by the 1920s, only certain phases of costume production were considered strictly women's work: those with domestic rather than artistic associations (for example, direct work with a needle and thread) that were of low status in the creative process and hierarchy, and that involved repetition of what might be called detail work such as embroidery, making use of women's "natural" dexterity, tidiness, and aptitude for carrying out routine tasks.[7]

Separated from the work of designing clothes, women in film production most often performed mechanized, low-paying labor similar to that of garment factory workers.[8] The overlooked, second-class work of film editing recalls how Bauhaus women artists were often relegated to the "women's work" of weaving. Vertov makes a visual argument for this connection in *Man with a Movie Camera* (his wife, film editor Elizaveta Svilova, edited and appeared as editor in the film).

The technological and historical connections between textiles and films provide a foundation for my interest here: namely, taking material and cultural contexts into consideration, how might we "read" the presence of fabric on film? Historians and theorists who have focused their work specifically on textiles offer intriguing perspectives on tactility, making, and aesthetics that are relevant to those working with a range of art forms. Reading the representation and usage of textiles in cinema provokes conversations across a range of disciplines, including fashion and film studies, and fields such as popular culture studies, gender studies, and craft studies. Topics in performance and media studies include detailed attention to the central role of props in cinema history, as well as investigations into the sensory experience of film audiences. Significantly absent from these discussions is a rigorous examination of the contributions of scholars working in textile studies.

Over the past few decades, those working in textile studies have seen their field grow and expand. Itself an interdisciplinary field, textile studies continues to build on its anthropological and art historical foundations to create a community uniquely attentive to theory and practice. Since the early 2000s, when I began my work in textile studies, I have been inspired by scholars who integrate textile-making with theory, history, and other forms of art and media. Publications and museum exhibits in the field continue to diversify and develop wide-ranging and provocative conversations. My experience with textile studies began at the University of Minnesota, where my interest in poetry and dress was enriched by the insights and wisdom of my graduate school English Department professors Drs. Paula Rabinowitz, Maria Damon, Jani Scandura, and Lois Cucullu. Dr. Rabinowitz encouraged me to take Dr. Joanne Eicher's class in African dress and culture at the U of M—this was an essential course in my learning about the field. Pairing my developing library in dress and textile studies with my ongoing readings in feminist literary thought, I found richly layered intersections and endless questions.

Because the study of textiles involves seeing the world through an intersectional lens—considering wide-ranging factors such as gender, class, ethnicity, the histories of science and technology, as well as other areas—I have found it useful to think of textiles as a complex frame through which we can examine film. Considering the role of textiles in any medium demands a simultaneous attention to the physical make-up of fabric as well as to its network of historical and cultural meanings. Reading film through textiles (and textiles through cinematic media) means reading in a way that redirects meaning to that which is often overlooked, including the representation of women and gender, behind-the-scenes labor, and architectural and bodily ornamentation.

Paying close attention to the social connotations of certain fabrics (such as polyester) and the material qualities of textiles (such as their tactility, light reflectivity, and ability to free, inhibit, or enhance movement) unearths new possibilities for close-reading cinematic texts. I assume, in my readings of textiles on film, that the physical properties of textiles are crucial to understanding their cultural meanings. Considering the characteristics of specific fabrics such as satin, and patterns such as black-and-white striping, has been central to my analysis. Additionally, the tactility of the textile, both in its remembered sensation and in its visual manifestation on screen, inspires analyses that include and interrogate the haptic.

Textiles are found throughout the mise-en-scène of films—in sets, as props, as well as in clothing and ornamentation—and are used by filmmakers to create mood, communicate meaning, and convey drama and suspense.[9] Fiber-based props, in conjunction with editing and cinematography, can create critical moments in the development of character and narrative. Rather than looking at films that document fashion styles and trends, I investigate the representation and impact of textiles in (primarily) fiction films. My focus often turns to objects of clothing, decoration, and interior design such as curtains, wall coverings, and other architectural elements. In addition to investigating fabric placed in front of the camera, I consider the way the camera and post-production editing utilize textiles—especially the physical behaviors and cultural associations of specific fabrics—to create a layered, dynamic screen. The memories and meanings we, as viewers, attach to textiles result in multilayered effects on-screen.

Historically, textiles have occupied space in cinema, from the camera lens to the sets, props, and costumes of film productions. Their presence is so common that sometimes they can be difficult to notice at all. Throughout this text I have tried to read films in a way that pays attention to what is unnoticed, not just in terms of what appears on screen, but in what textiles can suggest or comment on indirectly, particularly regarding questions of gender and labor. The lack of acknowledgment and respect for work typically performed by women, in industrial and in domestic settings, is a concern that drives many of my readings here. As this exploited labor is essential to the development of both the textile and film industries, I wanted to be sure my case studies were attentive to these conditions. My hope is that these readings will open up ideas about how to read texts in a way that makes fabric central. While this book is not a linear historical or chronological account, cultural and social histories, in addition to formal analysis, are foundational to my interpretations. Perhaps the questions I have begun to ask here will lead to further focused, historically informed studies within the fields of textile and film.

The following chapters include films selected because they make significant use of textiles or because some aspect of the film foregrounds textiles. Textiles have long been important in advancing visual stories; notably, some of the first visual narratives—tapestries—were fiber-based.[10] A film such as *The Cobweb* (dir. Vincente Minnelli, 1955) builds its tension around the purchase of drapes, a seemingly trivial detail that nonetheless propels the plot forward. The documentary *Clotheslines* (dir. Roberta Cantow, 1981) features images of clothes drying on lines in order to depict its examination of domestic work. *Gabbeh* (dir. Mohsen Makhmalbaf, 1996) follows the journey of a rug across generations and locations, narrating a story of personal history and cultural tradition. In these films, textiles exist to drive the plot—which may not necessarily concern fabric—forward. I am interested in imagining fabric on film as a catalyst for provoking cultural critique in addition to illustrating narrative action.

Seeing textiles on film as significant, including and beyond plot development, extends the possibilities for analysis farther than the diegetic world of film. Because many films labeled "experimental" do not rely on conventional Hollywood narrative strategies, mise-en-scène takes on increased prominence in these types of films. The ongoing interest in materiality and materialist thought in avant-garde film history has informed my perspective, and in the following chapters I have consciously placed readings of mainstream films alongside several lesser-known experimental films, to demonstrate their interrelation and mutual influence, despite their differing economic and cultural contexts. While the conditions of their making, particularly in terms of budget, differ significantly, both Hollywood and non-Hollywood films often use the same tools, technology, equipment, and points of reference.

The making of films and the making of textiles are both rooted simultaneously in craft and industry, and so recent conversations in craft studies about the role of industry in craft (and vice versa) have provided a useful touchpoint for this project. Glenn Adamson's discussion of the "industrial artisan" and his assertion that "[craft and industry] were created alongside one another, each defined against the other through constant juxtaposition," has been helpful in considering the interrelation of textiles and films.[11] I share Adamson's belief that instead of seeing craft as, as he writes, industry's "other," it is more useful to avoid these restrictive binary oppositions. Investigating textiles and film side by side rather than in a hierarchical relationship has proven productive, inspiring questions across disciplines.

As Bauhaus weaver Anni Albers notes, "modern industry is the new form of the old crafts, and both industry and the crafts should remember their genealogical relation. Instead of a feud, they should have a family reunion."[12] Kathleen Morris argues that the romanticizing of craft has further isolated us from the reality of craft work: "as Western countries have inched further away from pre-modern modes of production, craft has been cemented in the public imagination as a beloved symbol of the void left behind, commonly viewed through rose-colored glasses, and shrouded in nostalgia."[13] And T'ai Smith points out the need to "disrupt" the craft/industry binary: "almost nothing is purely one or the other."[14] Looking at industry and craft together forces us to consider the labor supporting both areas—and this demand for recognition among theorists is essential for my interdisciplinary look at textiles on film. My interest in examining textiles is rooted in a desire to resist detaching filmmaking and fabric-making from the labor that enables their production.

Those working in fields designated as craft are usually referred to as makers. It is important to note that definitions of "making" differ among textile scholars and those working in film studies. Film studies scholarship generally attributes the technical and aesthetic decisions in making a film to the filmmaker. Scholarship in film has long worked to move film into category of "high art" (to counter film's beginnings as a type of entertainment associated with mass culture and the working class). In part an emphasis on the film "auteur" (the film's principal visionary) has resulted in an erasure of the many other "makers" who are crucial to the development and production of a film. I am interested in exploring whether paying serious attention to the overlooked objects of film's mise-en-scène, and particularly those that do not appear to have a direct relation to the film's narrative progress, could help develop more widespread awareness of what has been overlooked in film and filmmaking.

Adamson claims, "it is precisely through an examination of the terms of [craft's] insubordination that the social prejudices that attend craft can be redressed."[15] And Naomi Schor argues that evaluating the ornamental detail can disrupt "an internal hierarchic ordering of the work of art which clearly subordinates the periphery to the center, the accessory to the principal, the foreground to the background."[16] Shifting our attention to what has long been marginalized, feminized, and degraded as mere "artifice" creates new avenues for questioning and discussion. Specifically, I am interested in how the rich history of fiber-based craft and the scholarly work of textile theorists have already disrupted this "internal hierarchic ordering." Extending the field of textile studies into other art forms reveals film's overlooked dependence on textiles, and shows how cinematic technology might reframe our sensory and cultural perceptions of cloth. Reading and writing in both textile studies and film studies have offered up seemingly endless areas of questioning and exploration. The joining of such provocative disciplines will surely lead to compelling new inquiry and research.

Textiles serve multiple purposes on film. Their movements and textures are particularly significant in relation to our bodies—they can steer the motion of our eyes around the composition of the screen, and they can develop a sense of tactility in a medium that is not (at least, not until the advent of touch screens) ordinarily defined by touch. As the field of textile studies has grown, film scholarship has experienced a parallel interest in materiality and the sensory experience of watching films (though not, to my knowledge, in reference to textile studies). Groundbreaking work by scholars such as Laura Marks and Vivian Sobchack examines the intersections of film, embodiment, and phenomenology. In this book I focus on visual and tactile experience, but also include, at times, references to sound and smell. Sobchack's compelling argument for including the "carnal foundations of cinematic intelligibility" in film studies is an important influence on my project. She speaks of film studies as "a discipline that has worked long and hard to separate the sense and meaning of vision and specularity from a body that, *in experience*, lives vision always in cooperation and significant exchange with other sensorial means of access to the world, a body that makes meaning before it makes conscious, reflective thought."[17]

My approach also relies on Marks's theory of "haptic visuality": compared with a more vision-centered cinematic experience, Marks says that "haptic looking tends to move over the surface of its object rather than plunge into illusionistic depth, not to distinguish form so much as to discern texture."[18] As surface and texture are essential characteristics of fabric, Marks's approach is important for my consideration of the specific contributions of fiber-based material to visual media.[19] As film scholars consider factors, such as the haptic, already essential to those who work in textile studies, textile scholars increasingly take on the structural and theoretical techniques familiar to film studies departments. I close-read the "language" of fabric while reframing it within relevant contexts, examining the technologies of the film camera as well as the cultural and historical conditions of the film and its featured textiles.

Works exploring affect theory—by writers such as Lauren Berlant, Sara Ahmed, and Sianne Ngai—have provided me with astute models of how to approach subject matter that alternates between the tangible and intangible. Many of the textiles I discuss here have strong affect—they provoke strong emotions, ranging from pleasure to disgust, in the viewer. Because my focus is on film, the audience's initial reaction to a textile on screen is often visual, though many fabrics can make visceral, tactile, and other types of sensory impact. Eugenie Brinkema's *The Forms of the Affects* intriguingly combines film studies, object theory, and formal analysis in a way that has been helpful to my thinking. While my study relies more on the tenets of textile studies and the anthropology of dress and fashion than on the philosophy of aesthetics, I appreciate Brinkema's linking of close-reading practices with ideas in affect theory. She writes in her preface: "this book's insistence on the formal dimension of affect allows not only for specificity but for the wild and many fecundities of specificity: difference, change, the particular, the contingent (*and*) the essential, the definite, the distinct, all dense details, and—again, to return to the spirit of Deleuze—the minor, inconsequential, secret, atomic."[20]

In focusing on what is often rejected as trivial—"the minor, inconsequential, secret, atomic"—I hope to introduce areas of inquiry that have been suppressed or marginalized. As Naomi Schor writes of her project in *Reading in Detail*: "to read in detail is, however tacitly, to invest the detail with a truth-bearing function, and yet [. . .] the truth value of the detail is anything but assured."[21] Sustained attention to detail, Schor explains, risks "the danger that to write *on* the detail is to become lost *in* it."[22] Like Schor, I take this risk, as I have found that it is often the "unassured" nature of the detail's "truth value" that inspires interpretation. Once the assumed definition of the detail's meaning begins to fall apart, we move toward unexpected, creative readings. For example, in writing the case studies for this book I have often found myself immersed in very specific details—the quality of light on a particular fabric, or the multifaceted experience of watching the movement of filmed curtains across a window—and these details have led me into different areas of study. Underlying my readings always are the histories, in aesthetic scholarship, of critiquing colonialist, capitalist, and patriarchal structures.

Always, too, my analysis is grounded in materiality and embodiment. The apparatus of film and textile technologies provide important context for my case studies.[23] Centering textiles in film analysis opens up intriguing questions about industry, labor, gender, and class status, and I am indebted to the writings of materialist philosophers such as Theodor Adorno and Walter Benjamin for my object-based, capitalism-critical approach. Taking into account material qualities, technological histories, and social connotations of various fabrics, I treat textiles as culturally and historically resonant objects of study.

In addition to provoking investigation into issues of work and class, textiles are also closely associated with domesticity, femininity, and women's labor, and consistently lead to fruitful conversations about visual gender expression. My chapters frequently incorporate discussions of women and work, both because of my dedication to these topics and because of their intimate connection to the history of textiles. Historically, fabric has played a significant role in the defining of queer identities and communities, and I return repeatedly to the issue of how textiles intervene in on-screen representations of cultural persecution and acceptance, particularly around questions of sexuality and femininity. I consider, too, how race, ethnicity, and class intervene in these conversations.

The interdisciplinary nature of textiles requires wide-ranging investigation: physical experience is important to consider alongside social and political meanings. I move, in the following chapters, between more literal considerations of fabric functionality and visual effect, and abstract examinations of cultural connotations of specific textiles. I am always interested, too, in the presence of the film screen—as a textile and as an additional layer of mediated communication. While my expertise in textile studies is not that of a chemist or preservationist, I find that continually returning to the materiality of fiber-based objects—in asking questions about their source, their production, their usage, and their historical role—has allowed me to build interpretations that consider the making of textiles, even as they may seem to blend into the background of a film set.

The films I investigate here were chosen for their ability to articulate and complicate the textile/film connection. My focus is mainly on films that feature textiles as part of how they develop their argument, their mood, and/or their narrative, rather than documentaries or films that depict textile production or fiber-based artisanal skill.[24] I am primarily concerned with close-reading the representation of textiles on the film screen. For this reason I am not, for the most part, dealing with video art pieces, museum installations, artist textiles, and art made with cinematic materials (such as Greg Climer's "knit film" or Sabrina Gschwandtner's "film quilts"), though I am certainly impacted by these provocative artworks, which are in many ways aligned with my viewpoint, especially in the commentaries they provide about media, labor, and materiality. Aside from my conclusion, where I speak about one of Jodie Mack's video pieces, I stick to films intended for traditional theatrical settings, though in contemporary life they may now be viewed on multiple types of electronic devices.

In addition, I am primarily looking at woven and knit fabrics (both handmade and machine-made), and, aside from a brief mention of fur, animal skins do not figure prominently in this study. The malleability, variety, and visual/tactile qualities of woven fabrics, as well as their significance within the history of industrial textile production, make them well-suited to my discussion of textiles mediated by film. The look and composition of woven cloth alternates between structures that reveal and hide their construction, and the varying looseness and tightness of the weave impact the way the textile hangs and moves. The visibility of the intersecting warp and weft affects how a viewer might read a particular textile; for example, in my first chapter, which examines satin on screen, the tight weave and floating threads of satin fabric allow the audience to forget that it is fabric and perhaps see it as a metallic or liquid element. A looser weave—an example is the fraying gauze curtains I discuss in Chapter 5—calls attention to woven fabric's construction and potential for decay.

Moving between examination of the sensory experience of specific fabrics and evaluation of their representation and social impact, in the following chapters I locate meanings that resonate physically, culturally, and emotionally. Roland Barthes calls dress "a kind of text without end"; while Barthes's focus is on fashion rather than textiles, his portrayal of an endlessly generative and readable field is accurate in describing my overall experience studying clothing, textiles, and fashion.[25] Among the issues I discuss in the following case studies are: how certain textiles provoke emotional reactions, such as desire and revulsion, in film viewers; how the permeable boundary between visuality and tactility creates tensions between the physical and the psychological, and between the immediate and the nostalgic; how filmmakers use framing and lens technology to develop suspense and direct the audience's awareness; how fabrics can transmit messages of social rebellion and sexual transgression as well as obfuscation and colonialist romanticizing; how reading "into" the surfaces presented on film complicates spatial intimacy and distance as well as depth and dimension; and how the semiotics of both textiles and film can be interpreted with attention to both disciplines.[26]

In my first chapter, "Modern Women Wear Satin: Fabric, Femininity, and Art Deco Hollywood," I examine a specific textile—satin—in a specific time period—the 1930s—to see how it illuminates our understanding of how women's bodies are figured on screen. Looking at the surfaces of textiles on the surface of the screen, I work to further uncover how nonverbal meaning unfolds on film. This chapter evaluates the way satin fabric reflects light on film, mirroring major concerns of the time. *Top Hat* (dir. Mark Sandrich, 1935), *Dancing Lady* (dir. Robert Z. Leonard, 1933), and other films from the '20s and '30s use satin in costuming to articulate "modern" views of gender, sexuality, class, and work. The shine on satin material and how it is enhanced with cinematographic technique contributes to my analysis of how women were portrayed as a type of coinage during an era of economic desperation. Satin and the shininess of Art Deco material on the film screen reflect the viewer/consumer's desires back to them, maintaining a state of capitalist longing.

"'That Polyester Look': Cinematic/Synthetic/Aesthetic" investigates the way a specific textile—polyester—can resonate with a film's aesthetic and political message. I show how artifice is rooted in the materiality of film and is explored in films that examine the synthetic through textiles.[27] My second chapter considers films from the 1970s such as *Saturday Night Fever* (dir. John Badham, 1977) that delve into issues surrounding class status, political awakening, and gender expression. A textile that often inspires revulsion, polyester evokes middle-class aspiration and the rise of synthetic materials in the twentieth century. On film, synthetic fabrics can express a more fluid version of gender and sexuality; *Polyester* (dir. John Waters, 1981) portrays a layered vision of women, domestic labor, and "tackiness."

The particular historical and cultural situation of polyester helps reframe the perceived "naturalness" of the housewife.

"Screen Prints: Striping and Cinematic Language," my third chapter, reads the specific themes of transgression and imprisonment evoked by stripes on film. Textiles are steeped in history and cultural-specific references at the same time as they are endlessly changeable in meaning. The process of how fabrics can accumulate new meaning while retaining traces of an older message is evident in the specific example of striping on the film screen. I discuss how patterning on textiles and on films can describe characters working through the restrictions and freedoms that accompany changing social perceptions. On screen, prints move across dress and architectural elements, and across geographical and historical spaces. I focus on how striping appears in films from various locales and time periods—in films such as *Black Girl* (dir. Ousmane Sembène, 1966), *Querelle* (dir. Rainer Werner Fassbinder, 1982), and *Mildred Pierce* (dir. Michael Curtiz, 1945), stripes take on various meanings according to their time and cultural place. Black-and-white striping reinforces the pattern's criminalized history while communicating details about mood and character.

Chapter 4, "Watching is Touching: On-Screen Transgression," explores how certain fabrics inspire a longing for tactile experience. Textiles reveal how a sense of touch heightens the audience's emotional engagement with the cinematic subject. Linking the desire to touch the screen with the desire to touch an object of unrequited love, I investigate the compulsive desire for velvet in *Blue Velvet* (dir. David Lynch, 1986). Taking into account other representations of taboo sexuality and transgression in relation to textiles, I also examine scenes from *In the Mood for Love* (dir. Wong Kar-wai, 2000), *It Happened One Night* (dir. Frank Capra, 1934), and *Pickpocket* (dir. Robert Bresson, 1959). Textiles work within the mise-en-scène as props, costuming, and bodily movement to approach and then move away from taboo subject matter, creating drama and suspense. Often unspoken, these forbidden relationships can be articulated in the suggestive choreography between actors and textiles. This dance of closeness and distance, often depicted around and with textiles, communicates a sense of prohibited tactility. In the later part of this chapter I examine how the physical positioning and placement of fabrics within a scene illuminate the dynamics among audience, screen, and the world of the film.

In my fifth chapter, "Moving Pictures: Magic, Suspense, and Textiles in Motion," I employ a seemingly insignificant detail—draped fabric in motion—to examine how the surfaces of the cinematic mise-en-scène take on significance. Fabric's unique ability to hide and reveal helps explain the role of moving cloth in developing suspense and mystery. In addition to creating suspense, this imagery articulates the condition of erotic frustration and the transformative "magic" of filmmaking itself. While gesturing to theatrical performance, the presence of curtains can also be used for impact. Blowing curtains can suggest uncertainty, longing, foreboding, introspection, and fear, among other emotions, to build mood and atmosphere. These textiles help create a sense of suspense in films such as *Rebecca* (dir. Alfred Hitchcock, 1940). *Black Narcissus* (dir. Michael Powell and Emeric Pressburger, 1947) presents us with a perpetually windy environment where moving curtains track the growing instability of the characters. As many film narratives rely on the development of plot intrigue and audience anticipation, the motif of fabric blown by a wind source shows how textiles help create mood, develop character emotion, and give the screen dimension and tactility.

1

Modern Women Wear Satin

Fabric, Femininity, and Art Deco Hollywood

The film screen presents us with multiple layered surfaces. The screen itself is a surface, and the surfaces of sets, props, and costuming make up the visual world of the film. As our eyes move across these surfaces, the qualities of light and texture direct and capture our attention. Satin fabric, a material that evokes urbanity and glamour, possesses a unique relationship with light and the film camera. In this chapter I am concerned with how satin complicates ideas about women, femininity, and class in 1930s Hollywood film. The idea of the modern woman, often expressed in the metallic and lacquered surfaces of Art Deco interiors and statuary, is brought to life by the satin-clad Hollywood film starlet.

The physical properties of satin are relevant to understanding the broad cultural and political themes present in the films I discuss here. In particular, I see the relationship between satin fabric and the cinematographer's use of light as contributing significantly to the representation of the modern woman's body in a time of rapid technological development as well as economic crisis. The specific components of satin presented filmmakers with a novel way to direct light and focus the viewer's eye. In a satin weave, the weft threads float over the warp, creating a surface of "floats." Satin fabrics, Elena Phipps writes, "are particularly lustrous due to the ability of the long float to reflect light."[1]

Originally made in China from silk, satin has historically been seen as delicate, expensive, and associated with wealth. The delicacy of interweaving satin threads perpetuates its status as a coveted textile: satin is "a weave structure with a surface of long floats, bound in a systematic way, but whose binding is not readily visible. Satin fabrics, often made of silk, are particularly lustrous due to the ability of the long float to reflect light. However, if the float is too long, the woven structure loses its integrity."[2] Fragile, beautiful, and difficult to acquire, satin's origins established its rarity and desirability. Unlike most textiles, satin conceals its warp and weft, an effect that renders its maker invisible and further separates this fabric from the working class. Anni Albers writes of satin weave: "the long, floating threads cover the points of intersection of warp and weft and permit the threads to be beaten together closely, so that a uniform, smooth surface is achieved, lacking any obviously visible structural effects."[3] Satin's lack of a visible structure reinforces the idea that satin is a "magical" or "special" fabric, able to erase evidence of its making and take on the qualities of other materials (such as glass or chrome). Eventually, developments in synthetic textiles made satin more affordable to larger sections of the population.

The construction of satin fabric—with its floating warp and smooth, glossy look—catches and holds light in a more concentrated manner than other textiles. In descriptions of fiber-based objects specifically, luster is defined as a "gloss or sheen of a textile or fiber created through the reflectance of light on its surface."[4] The light seems to gather and pool on the finish of the fabric. The effect is often a kind of liquifying of the light, as if light has taken on a thicker, more tangible form. Satin's luster can recreate the look of melting metal, and is therefore especially effective, on film, in illustrating the layered relations between money, machines, and women's bodies.

Smooth and reflective, satin can look metallic on screen, offering unique opportunities for cinematographers. The strong, carefully directed bulbs on film sets control the directionality of light on satin in a way that focuses, rather than diffuses, light. This means that film viewers can visually track light as it moves on satin fabric. Often, light on satin is in continuous motion. A concentrated pool of light on satin's surface can act like a spotlight or multiple spotlights, guiding the eye.[5] Satin was and is sometimes still associated with bedroom décor, bridal wear, and lingerie. Because satin is most often used in domestic interiors and in women's dress, viewers are encouraged to follow moving light as it travels over women's bodies and intimate living spaces.

The visual eroticism of satin material is determined primarily by the fit of the garment on the body. It is often the dressmakers' decisions about fold and drape that dictate how exactly satin hugs the body. The new fashions in draped fabric popularized by designers Madeleine Vionnet and Madame Grès in the 1930s, as well as an aesthetic interest in classicism, for example in the dance costuming of Isadora Duncan, brought new focus to how different fabrics conformed to women's bodies, and, in turn, how these fabrics translated to the projected image. The tightness or looseness of the garment changes how our eye moves across the surface of the actor's body on screen.[6] Satin's role in creating draping effects—in the development of the bias cut, for example—contributes to this new presentation of the body. Satin material offered directors a way to visually emphasize athleticism and flexibility.[7]

Women's fashion in the early twentieth century was largely defined in opposition to the corset.[8] While the figure of the New Woman freed women's bodies from the restriction of the corset, it introduced new limitations. The vision of the modern American woman at this time was often a wealthy white woman who engaged in sporty leisure activities requiring flexible, loose clothing. In formal wear, satin marked its wearers as fashionable, and film helped popularize this notion.[9] By the 1920s and '30s, particularly in the United States, film had become a regular part of many people's lives. Movie attendance was high during The Great Depression of the 1930s, and a large population of the United States went to the movie theatre at least once weekly. In this era, a new story about changing attitudes about women and sexuality, as well as attitudes about money and class, unfurled on the film screen.

Fred Astaire and Ginger Rogers are famous for their graceful and physically challenging dance routines. They made many popular films in the 1930s, throughout the duration of and the recovery from The Great Depression. Their films are recognizable not only for their impressive dancing but for the sparkling, glittering sets and costumes on screen. Mirrored surfaces reflect light back to the camera, especially in elaborate, fantastical settings for dance numbers. Satin, alongside other types of ornamentation—such as sequined fabrics, lacquered floors, and mirrored walls—transforms the screen into a shining surface.

Materials such as cut glass, polished chrome, mirrors, and satin work together to develop a canvas in which the viewer's eye constantly follows light in motion. At this time, the act of watching light moving over women's bodies had taken on new anxiety. Censorship laws in accordance with the 1934 Hayes Code prevented overt discussion of sex on film: outrage over "morality" in 1920s and early 1930s films led to this code, which was developed in part by Hollywood studies. The code required that certain protocols were observed in order for films to be screened in US film theaters. In the UK, the British Board of Film Classification served a similar role. In order to get around these strict rules, filmmakers had to figure out different ways to express taboo topics. One of these, the restriction on showing an unmarried couple sleeping in the same bedroom, resulted in a creative use of hanging cloth in the 1934 film *It Happened One Night*, which I discuss in Chapter 4.

Satin and other elements of the mise-en-scène also helped to communicate unspoken desire during this era of censorship. Because the Astaire/Rogers film plots usually center around the marriage contract, nervousness about sex and desire often finds expression in nonsensical narratives, comical misunderstandings, and sparkling film sets.[10] Lucy Fischer writes,

> the Astaire/Rogers cycle was known for its 'integration' of narrative and production number. This stylistic unity followed from the fact that the films were essentially romantic comedies in which the love affair that blossomed between the leads was articulated through choreography. If, in the 'screwball comedy,' witty repartée functioned as a substitute for lovemaking, in the Astaire/Rogers musical that role fell to dance.[11]

We trace the characters' "blossoming" love affair through choreography as well as through the sparkling sets and the movement of light.

In Astaire/Rogers films, as in other notable films of the period by Busby Berkeley and Ernst Lubitsch, a glittering film screen, spectacular costuming, and quick dialogue are more important than a clear plotline. The emphasis on mise-en-scène rather than depth of character or complexity of narrative creates a palette that both stimulates the eye and flattens the screen space. Directors create an attitude toward watching film that is not unlike watching a beautifully draped gown—admiring, inspired, and transported. It is significant that this sort of escapist viewing experience was popular during this time. Many of these films were made and shown during The Great Depression, when a quarter of the population was unemployed. Films that presented worlds where characters did not worry about money, and where Hollywood's extravagant budgets could enable impressive props and luxurious costuming, were popular forms of temporary relief for many moviegoers.

Figure 1.1 Fred Astaire and Ginger Rogers dancing in *Top Hat*, 1935. Courtesy Getty Images U.K.

While the glittering, moneyed world of Hollywood fiction films likely did offer a sense of escape for film audiences at this time, this same world also serves to heighten the intense desire for economic security many viewers of the time must have felt. Diverging from readings that position Astaire/Rogers films as escapist, I see the mise-en-scène of these movies operating as a sort of mirror, reflecting the viewers' capitalist longing back to them. In the Astaire/Rogers films, there is no respite from the obsessive display of wealth and consumerism. It is as if viewers are trapped inside the feeling of shopping for things they will never be able to afford.[12]

The Rogers/Astaire films, unlike other films of the period (such as Busby Berkeley musicals), are not explicit about the political reality of their time and do not claim to be anything other than fantasy. The films are easy to watch, and the narratives do not require much thought. On Lubitsch, François Truffaut writes, "there is no Lubitsch plot on paper, nor does the movie make any sense after we've seen it. Everything happens *while* we are looking at the film."[13] This is also true for one of the most well-known of the Rogers-Astaire musicals, *Top Hat* (1935). Dale Tremont (Rogers) and Jerry Travers (Astaire) meet in London, where a series of humorous misunderstandings and musical numbers drive the narrative of their developing romance. The constant presence of mirrored materials and the denial of any outside reality forces the audience into a closed world, where their desire for escape is reflected back to them over and over. While *Top Hat* does not mention the Depression directly, its focus is consistently on money and wealthy display. In part its mise-en-scène works to repeatedly remind audiences they have no access to the world on the screen.

In *Top Hat*, light and satin help create the world of the film as a space of capitalist longing. An early scene uses satin to establish the sexual tension between Dale and Jerry. We are introduced to Jerry's hotel room, which is noteworthy for its modern décor: low horizontal lines; cut glass decanters; an angular pattern on the parquet floor; and small bright lights illuminating the rooms. As Jerry and Dale engage in banter, the camera moves closer to the actors and then moves back while Jerry dances, maintaining sparkling, light-filled compositions. The spectator's eye is pulled around the room and back to the actors' bodies in a way that feels smooth and constant. Catching on objects,

Figure 1.2 Fred Astaire dancing in *Top Hat*, 1935. Courtesy Getty Images U.K.

light moves around the screen in a manner similar to the movement of light on the surface of satin.

The central plot point of the scene is that Jerry's dancing is disturbing Dale, who is trying to sleep in the hotel room directly below him. Her presence is revealed when the scene cuts to her room.

The camera appears to move down to reveal a cutaway of the hotel, but the cut is actually a very brief dissolve. The appearance of tilting downward flattens the space of the film, an effect that emphasizes the film's theatricality: the film identifies itself as a fantastical construction, something which has been built. The viewer's eye moves freely between hotel rooms, peering in as if we are looking inside a dollhouse. The characters' trivial problems and minor annoyances with each other contribute to the sense that they are playing entertaining, doll-like roles for the audience.

We see Dale in her hotel suite, where the walls, bed, and Dale herself are all draped in satin fabric. Dale's platinum hair gleams like satin, and she pulls on a dressing gown with long heavy satin sleeves. When Dale leaves the room to complain about the noise, it looks as if her body has detached from the fabric covering her room. As we are acquainted with Dale in her room, we crosscut to Jerry dancing and looking at himself in an oval mirror. Both actors are presented as physically immersed in their reflective surroundings. Their bodies, especially Dale's, appear almost sunken into the shiny, mirrored material around them.[14] When they dance, it is as if they are decorative objects that have become animated. At one point, Dale catches Jerry dancing with a statue. This foregrounds Dale's eventual role as Jerry's dance partner—a piece of Art Deco statuary come to life.

Art Deco is a movement associated with consumerism and capitalist progress, and so it makes sense this is the style shown most prominently in *Top Hat*.[15] Satin embodies many of the ideals of the Art Deco movement. Art Deco innovations spanned, among other areas, architecture, fashion, and interior design, making material culture central to the study of this period. An emphasis on shine in particular made metal and lacquered surfaces an important part of the manufacture of Art Deco objects. While the materials of Art Deco architecture and décor—for example, the significant use of metals and glass—have been widely researched and examined, the role of satin in

Art Deco has received little attention. Other than Deco print designs on fabric, textiles are usually not included in conversations about the aesthetics of this period.

Attention to the use of satin on the film screen expands our understanding of Art Deco to include a broader range of materials and media. As discussed, the fashions of the time appear alongside mirrored and lacquered surfaces to create an overall shine effect on screen. This shininess, coupled with the draping techniques developed by Grès and Vionnet, create a dynamic canvas on which to manipulate light. The presence of satin on the film screen extends the Art Deco aesthetic beyond architectural and interior details, giving voice and movement to ideas about progress and modernity.

Specifically, women's bodies, often present as static in Art Deco décor, are brought to life when draped with satin on Art Deco-themed film sets. Fischer explains Art Deco's "fixation on the figure of the woman" as expressing the "ambivalence" society felt about the New Woman.[16] The "New Woman" usually refers to a post–First World War rejection of the Victorian puritanical view of women, a view also reflected in Art Deco styling, which stripped interiors of Victorian clutter and excessive decoration. In the relatively new medium of film, the New Woman embodies Art Deco's celebration of speed, athleticism, and the potential for transformation in the modern age.

It is important to note that the ideal future, as envisioned by Art Deco, is restricted to white women.[17] On film, white satin gowns not only provide visual interest but also reinforce the whiteness of the (usually white) celebrities wearing them. Art Deco design was notorious for its embrace by fascists and Nazis, and its classical references are punctuated with images that reflect the Orientalist and Primitivist trends of the period. While satin fabric is not as ideologically charged as other elements of Art Deco material culture, there are examples of the use of black satin as code for "bad" women. For example, in the 1935 film *Roberta* (dir. William A. Seiter), another Astaire/Rogers film, the plot revolves around a black satin dress made by Roberta, a fashion designer. The female characters use the dress, initially discarded for being too revealing, as they compete for the attentions of desirable bachelor John. The black satin marks its wearer as unmarriageable and therefore determines whom John will ultimately choose as his love interest. In *Pandora's Box* (dir. G.W. Pabst, 1929), the femme fatale Lulu at first wears white satin as she seduces and then marries her wealthy lover; when she appears on trial for his murder, she wears black satin. While many of the films of this period are noteworthy for their absence of any discussion or representation of racial diversity, the association of "blackness" with danger and threat reflects the unspoken racist attitude present in the worlds of these films.

Pandora's Box does not confront the issue of skin color, but it does make intriguing visual connections between satin and skin. At the beginning of the film, we see Lulu through her lover Schön's eyes: lying back on a bed, her neck and décolletage are lit at an angle so her skin appears as satiny as the sheen on the fabric of her dress. The painting hanging above her features a harlequin dancer wearing a shiny white satin suit, enhancing the appeal of Lulu's skin as she tells the engaged-to-be-married Schön that he will have to kill her to get rid of her. Lulu's body serves as an object of exchange several times in the film's narrative, as she is traded for money or sexual currency. Her body is bought and sold, and she never seems to be in complete possession of it. Over the course of the film, Lulu is portrayed repeatedly destroying the lives of those around her (in this way she is similar to the femme fatale character in *A Fool There Was*, which I discuss in Chapter 3). At the same time, her numerous seductions and manipulations of others do not bring her any power or influence.

Pandora's Box emerges from Weimar Germany, not, like the Astaire-Rogers films, from Hollywood, and the cultural and political contexts around sexuality are different. The Weimar period in cinema history

Figure 1.3 Louise Brooks as Lulu, wearing white satin on the set of *Pandora's Box*, 1929. Courtesy Getty Images U.K.

refers to the interwar years in Germany, when financial anxieties and artistic and sexual experimentation resulted in innovative and influential film productions. Mary Ann Doane writes of "the tendency of Weimar society in general to test continually the limits of sexuality

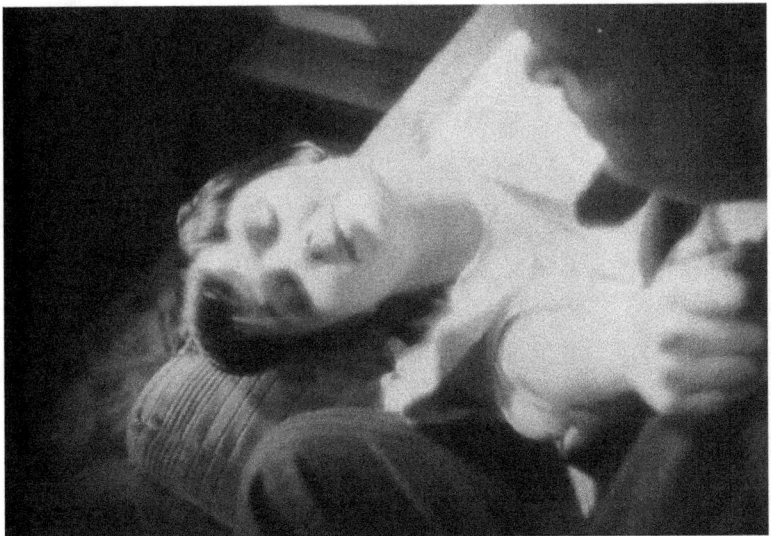

Figure 1.4 Louise Brooks as Lulu. Credit: *Pandora's Box* (dir. G.W. Pabst, 1929), Praesens Film AG.

in relation to legal (or moral) jurisdiction."[18] In *Pandora's Box* Lulu constantly moves against and away from the moralizing of her social circles, alternating between positions of power and vulnerability. Despite speaking from an environment more open to discussion of sexual difference, contemporary critics of Pabst dismissed his "obsession with surfaces and atmosphere" and "the decorative."[19]

Lulu's status as a "New Woman" and flapper (in other words, a woman who embraces changing ideas about sex and power in the 1920s) does not give her lasting control or influence in her society. Instead, she is continually "traded" among powerful men. As the figure of the woman in Art Deco is lifted up as the symbol of modernity and forward movement, at the same time she is reduced to a form of currency. In the United States, the link between surface and sexuality is portrayed more directly in pre-Hayes Code Hollywood. The qualities of satin fabric highlight issues of sexual subversion and power in films made before the establishment of the code. Mick LaSalle says,

Figure 1.5 Louise Brooks as Lulu, confronting Schön (Fritz Kortner), 1929. Courtesy Getty Images U.K.

the best era for women's pictures was the pre-Code era, the five years between the point that talkies became widely accepted in 1929 through July 1934, when the dread and draconian Production Code became the law of Hollywoodland. Before the Code, women on screen took lovers, had babies out of wedlock, got rid of cheating husbands, enjoyed their sexuality, held down professional positions without apologizing for their self-sufficiency, and in general acted the way many of us think women acted only after 1968.[20]

I would argue that pre-Code films are not entirely liberating—in fact many of them present a mixed message about women. In the pre-Code *Dancing Lady* (1933), the modern woman is figured as a type of coinage while also displaying agency and ambition. Joan Crawford plays Janie Barlow, a dancer who wants to get out of burlesque work and into dancing on the Broadway stage. Janie spends much of the film alternating between two high-powered men who exercise their control while expressing a confusing mix of love and disdain for Janie. The shining satin fabric so prevalent in the fashions of this time reinforces the sense that women are powerful primarily in their role as objects of exchange. Tracing the use of fabric in Janie's costuming shows how satin in particular communicates Janie's transition from economic desperation into financial stability. Always at stake in the narrative is the role Janie's body—both as a dancer and as a potential lover—will play in determining whether she succeeds. The shininess of her costuming throughout reinforces the idea that her body operates as a kind of currency.

At the start of the film Janie is arrested for lewd dancing at a strip club and is bailed out by a wealthy suitor who was slumming at the club. Her suitor, Tod Newton, gives her fifty dollars and advice on how to change her dress and language to appear less working class. In the apartment she shares with another burlesque dancer, we see Janie struggling with whether she should follow Tod uptown and seek societal approval for her dancing. She confesses her true ambitions to her skeptical roommate: Janie wants to be a legitimate dancer. Janie says she is through with burlesque and wants to go uptown, where dancing is considered "art." We see her ambition and, although she is insulted by Tod's attempts to change and control her, Janie decides to pursue dancing opportunities uptown.

After shutting off the lights, Janie undresses in front of the window. Outside, a neon light flashes on and off. The presence of flickering neon outside their apartment, likely in an undesirable downtown New York City location, underlines their marginalized economic status. The repeated flashing light also echoes Janie's persistent distaste for her working-class life and her anxious desire to get out. As this is a pre-Code film, the on-and-off motion of the light also provides a peek-a-boo look at Janie's body as she undresses. First, the outline of her satin-clad body is highlighted as she leans into the window. After this, we see her silhouette, the neon light behind her, at the center of the screen. Interestingly, this occurs at the moment of Janie's strongest assertion of ambition and willpower. As we look at the outline of her body, she voices her determination to create legitimacy and independence for herself. The fact that this legitimacy is linked to an already-established financial dependency between herself and Tod shows us that she has been caught in an exchange relationship and must spend the rest of the film attempting to sort this out. The pointed focus on her body demonstrates that it is her body which is at stake here and which will be at the center of this exchange, both in her dance career and in her role as object of sexual desire.

Immediately after this scene we are subject to a barrage of images, sounds, and editing techniques such as a whip pan and a fast tracking shot, intended to convey the speed with which Janie is traveling uptown. We are first in the subway, racing past signs marking different stops, and then find ourselves immediately at the stage door. This sequence makes a parallel between Janie's determination and modern transportation and photographic technologies. The linking of transportation with speed and modern life is found through films of the period; an important example is the pre-Code *Flying Down to Rio* (dir. Thornton Freeland, 1933), another Astaire-Rogers vehicle. This musical romance celebrates air travel as the pinnacle of modernity, displaying unusual Art Deco-styled wipes and split screen effects to transition between scenes, as well as a finale number featuring gravity-defying dancers performing on airplane wings.

We follow Janie's rise to success and the narrative eventually culminates in a production number that celebrates Janie as a transformed modern woman. In the "Rhythm of the Day" finale, the story turns on the visual transition of the stage from an "old-fashioned," slow-moving group of people in a Baroque setting to a new, modern Art Deco world. Film editors insert a vertical split at the center of the stage to show aesthetic, technological, and cultural transformation. As actors move from one side of the screen to the other, the costume, props, and background design undergo a dramatic change. Horse-drawn carriages are turned into cars, and speed and jazzy music become an essential part of the environment. Janie emerges from the car in a satin gown, surrounded by dancers in risqué costumes. A group of older women go to a "Beauty Repair Shop" where they are turned into "newer models." City backgrounds such as this one, Marketa Uhlirova writes, provides a "prime sites of modernity": "ever-evolving visual (and aural) landscapes that provide ideal landscapes against which fashion and film are staged."[21]

In the modern setting, the fast-paced point of view continues to rely on the figure of the woman as commodified object in need of "repair." Janie emerges from the narrative as a "new model," now wearing the classy satin gown of an uptown lady, having discarded the satin lingerie of her former working-class life. Esther Leslie, through Georg Simmel, links lighting, fashion, and the modern metropolis by connecting the "intensified level of sensory stimulation" of fashion and cinema to "an overflow of stimuli [intrinsic] to modern life itself."[22] As an uptown woman in a scintillating urban setting, Janie now projects this type of light-filled glamour. She has negotiated

Figure 1.6 Promotional poster for *Flying Down to Rio* (dir. Thornton Freeland, 1933), featuring dancers on a moving airplane. Courtesy Getty Images U.K.

her way to legitimacy, though she remains stuck as a piece of shiny currency exchanged between powerful men.

As previously mentioned, the shine on satin gives it a metallic look, and metals—especially chrome—are associated with futuristic Art

Deco design. The metal of cars, planes, and other machinery have the smooth, lustrous look of satin.[23] The quality of light created by satin and metal differs from the shininess of glitter and sequins. Glitter, sequins, glass, rhinestones, and other faceted, jeweled surfaces scatter light, reflecting and fracturing light away from themselves, often suggesting a magical, singular moment. The starburst or pointillist effect—which throws dots of light in a sort of spray toward the camera lens—can illustrate a sense of otherworldliness or fleetingness.[24] Satin also reflects, rather than absorbs, light. Instead of catching light and throwing it back in flecks and fragments to the viewer, satin holds light, creating a more concentrated (and metallic-looking) optical effect.

Across historical and cultural lines, the use of light reflection in dress and ornament is an effective way to communicate economic value. Victoria Rivers writes that "civilizations all around the world assign great value to cloths and items of personal adornment which use light-reflecting materials," and that "much human endeavor, energy, and expense are devoted to the creation of stunning, lavish, and imaginative light-reflecting textiles, although they are hardly essential to survival."[25] Though shiny textiles themselves are not necessary to survive, the object they reference and celebrate— money—is of course crucial to survival.[26] The seductive image of the woman, especially those glowing with an Art Deco shine, express the physical and psychological longings of capitalist culture.[27]

However, the figure of a commodified, metallic-looking woman can also edge toward representations of horror and monstrosity. The 1927 film *Metropolis*, directed by Fritz Lang, another Weimar director, is often held up as the pinnacle of Art Deco set design. The film's noteworthy mise-en-scène is the setting for a moral fable that confronts wealth and privilege and the plight of industrial workers. Maria, the primary female character, is depicted as simultaneously a compassionate, maternal savior figure and a demonic robot unleashing the worst of capitalist industrialist greed. Played by the same actress, Brigitte Helm, the human Maria and her robot counterpart (created in Maria's image) are a particularly straightforward example of how metallic material and femininity combine to create a vision of modern horror. When the mad scientist Rotwang brings his metal robot form to life, she has the face of the angelic Maria but is a heartless and chaos-provoking machine.

Karl Toepfer says of *Metropolis*: "no other film has ever used dance, costume and cinematic technique to produce such a complicated emotional response from the viewer and make such a complex statement about the relation between technology and sexuality."[28] The robot Maria's seductive dance in a men's nightclub brings about rioting and destruction in the city (similarly, *Pandora's Box* explores the figure of the woman who incites chaos). Dangerous and desired, the machine/woman is capable of inciting chaotic transformation. Fears about technology often find expression on the film screen; during the first half of the century in particular, before widespread use of color processing, the visual effect of metal is well-suited to the cinematography of the time as well as to imagined visions of a technological future.

More recently, films such as *Under the Skin* (dir. Jonathan Glazer, 2013) utilize digital special effects to, in the tradition of *Metropolis*, create a terrifying combination of beautiful woman and inhuman alien/robot. In this film the transitions from reality into an otherworldly dimension are marked by the presence of a digitally enhanced environment. The narrative revolves around what Ara Osterweil calls "the female protagonist's ritual seductions": "driving around Scotland while gazing through the window of her van, she picks up random male passerby, and lures them to a distant site where they are conveniently disemboweled in a viscous lagoon."[29] As the protagonist seduces her male victims, they sink into an often colorless

Figure 1.7 Robot Maria (Brigitte Helm)'s face as she incites chaos among male viewers with her provocative dancing. Courtesy Getty Images UK.

space. Somewhere between solid and liquid, this environment acts like the malleable metal of the morphing, dangerous woman.[30]

While *Under the Skin* does not make explicit use of satin fabric, the metallic shine of the alien's world recalls the qualities of satin. The deadly "viscous lagoon" shines like satin; the use of concentrated, pooling light is another satin-like feature of *Under the Skin*. In the film, gleaming surfaces are figured as seductive. Like the femme fatale characters in *Pandora's Box* and *Metropolis*, the alien woman in this film is predatory and destructive. A seductive and manipulative "monster," she uses men's fixations on her body in order to prey on them. Throughout, we are presented with a series of void-like spaces as well as an ocean drowning—mirrored surfaces that bewitch victims and pull them under. The alien's lure, seemingly connected to the landscape, serves as a warning about the attractive sheen of late capitalism: rather than promising the hope of a modern future, as seen in Art Deco-styled sets, *Under the Skin* offers a vision of horror.

The film's sleek surfaces, associated with the alien, suggest a cold metal world in opposition to reality. In making significant use of the properties of metal, including its liquid quality when unformed, the filmmaker depicts the processes of making, both in craft and in industry, as alien and alienated from the characters' lives. It is the liquid form of metal that envelops the victims, suggesting they are returning to some sort of unformed state. Created using computer technology, the images of men sinking into the liquid presents an eerie vision of total disappearance. This specific aspect of the film's mise-en-scène—the motif of both melted and hardened metal—echoes earlier films which link women and commodification as a response to technological development and economic change.

The qualities of satin—its metallic, liquid appearance and association with women and sexuality—has made for evocative costuming and set design. At a time of financial collapse, the Hollywood studios of the 1930s offered up silvery reflections of wealth and comfort to its audiences. Shiny materials presented on screen act as mirrors, continually reflecting audience's (usually cash-strapped) reality back to them. Futuristic Art Deco sets and costuming move light—and the viewer's eye—around the screen, highlighting modern women and modern technology. Characters restricted by set social roles and science-fiction visions of robotic, unfeeling femmes fatales convey a darker, more fearful side of how women are seen within this mise-en-scène. Reading satin and satin-like surfaces as they appear through the camera lens brings focus to how a particular fabric illuminates meaningful background elements on screen.

The idea that a single fabric type can absorb, alter, and disseminate cultural information, particularly in representations of gender, class, and power, is a central concern of my next chapter, which explores the look and connotations of polyester and other synthetic fabrics. Both satin and polyester fabric were marketed as cutting-edge fabrics, designed to meet the needs and desires of their forward-thinking buyers. Like satin, polyester offered the public a vision of the future in which a machine-made textile might transform their lives. The historical trajectory of polyester, however, moved from a celebration of its high-tech origins to a rejection of its tackiness and lack of connection to modern culture. Imagery projected on the film screen embodied and reframed perceptions of what was new, what was "natural," and what was potentially threatening.

2

"That Polyester Look"

Cinematic/Synthetic/Aesthetic

Sifting through used clothes in thrift stores, I find synthetic fabrics offer up a wide range of textures. Older, more cheaply made polyester garments feel scratchy and make a sound when I drag my fingernails across them. Other 100 percent polyester clothes are smooth—almost like satin—to the touch. Many appear to be soft and luxurious, but often you have to touch them to know for sure. The resemblance between polyester and silk on screen helps create a visual illusion—a fabric that in reality is inexpensive could look luxurious and costly. Polyester is particularly cost-efficient for film costumers, as, especially in its more high-quality forms, it looks very similar to silk.[1]

Speaking about polyester fabric immediately provokes an emotional reaction. Most often, this emotion is some shade of revulsion. Whether recoiling at its stiff, scratchy feel, laughing at its gauche sensibility, or being embarrassed by its cheapness and lower-class associations, we experience visceral reactions to this cloth. Consumers and practitioners dislike polyester for its associations with tackiness and its lack of sensory appeal. As fabric manufactured for clothing, polyester has moved from being celebrated (in the mid-late twentieth century) for its efficiency and convenience, to being mocked for its discomfort and "unnaturalness." This chapter is concerned with reading the cultural and emotional language of polyester and, more broadly, synthetic fabrics. The films I discuss in this chapter occasionally present compelling examples of polyester as props and costuming; their main points of interest, however, lie in the way they present us with a multisensory, multidimensional articulation of polyester's role in society.

Emerging from the technological invention that produced nylon, and providing the foundation for future synthetics such as spandex, polyester's impact has been significant. In his study of the influential DuPont chemical company, Pap Ndiaye points out DuPont's crucial role in "both synthetic fibers (nylon) and nuclear components (plutonium)," and how "in the 1950s, nylon symbolized a new way of life, the future, the spirit of America and its mythical modernity."[2] Nylon and its increasing numbers of polymer cousins (such as polyester) represented a sense of post–Second World War optimism at the same time as they presented new environmental dangers. Polyester and other synthetic textiles were practical and resilient, with good elasticity and uncomplicated washing instructions. The affordability and malleability of nylon in the 1920s and 1930s, Rachel Worth notes, "made it attractive to the ready-to-wear industry, and it offered men and women on modest incomes an opportunity to enjoy mainstream fashions at affordable prices."[3]

The reduced labor required for consumers to care for synthetic fabrics was an important selling point; in addition, the ability of these textiles to be manufactured inexpensively was crucial to their success. Worth writes,

> In the period after the Second World War, Marks & Spencer technologists were preoccupied with introducing new, commercially viable fabrics as population increased and living standards slowly began to improve following the economic dislocation caused by the war. Natural fabrics such as cotton, linen and wool—though in high demand—were exhaustible and the perceived advantages of man-made and synthetic alternatives lay in their lower price potential and easy-care qualities.[4]

Over time, the mass production associated with synthetic fabric eventually marked it as unfashionable: Susannah Handley writes, "the very proliferation of polyester was its downfall."[5] Though polyester has become a laughable textile, the current iteration of popular synthetic fabric—especially in "athleisure" clothing—shares a chemical history with early synthetics.[6]

The manufacture of polyester in particular grew in conjunction with an increasingly globalized textile industry (especially in the latter half of the twentieth century). *The Man in the White Suit* (dir. Alexander Mackendrick, 1951) is an important film for understanding anxieties around synthetic fiber, especially in the UK. The growing popularity of polyester was central in blurring the rigid lines that separated economic groups. A fiction film about the textile industry (though not necessarily about the representation of textiles), the Ealing satire *The Man in the White Suit* imagines a magical fabric that poses a threat to the capitalist textile industry. Of the film, Susannah Handley says:

> *The Man in the White Suit* was, in reality, symptomatic of many of the attendant worries of the sudden chemical-fibre revolution. Nothing would ever be the same again: textile making, clothing manufacture, retailing, dry cleaning, and, most confusing of all, the social status and value attached to fabrics and fashion. Would an everlasting suit be the dream or the nightmare of modern man? This was the cultural background against which polyester was set.[7]

Among polyester's assets was the fact that it did not demand additional housework such as ironing.[8] For this reason, the birth of polyester, and the subsequent incorporation of synthetics into everyday life, make polyester a provocative touchpoint for discussing consumption and culture in the mid-late twentieth century.[9] Women, often associated with domestic labor, have been important consumers of synthetic fabrics from the initial production of DuPont nylon in the late 1930s. Susan Smulyan writes, "as the company interacted with the women who bought nylon stockings, DuPont constructed what it meant to be gendered humans as well as gendered consumers in the twentieth century."[10] From the beginning, the making and usage of synthetic fabrics have intertwined with issues of gender and labor.

As I show in several films from the 1970s, a changing perception of what it means to be a housewife finds expression in the presentation of fabrics on film. Historically, the housewife of the 1950s is presented as celebrating the relief that synthetics brought to domestic labor. Polyester is linked to the growing middle-class suburbs in post–Second World War United States, and its usage altered the mechanics of daily household work. As growing feminist movement begins to question the role of "housewife," polyester on film reflects a new perception of women and work. Societal attitudes toward new synthetic fabrics (as toward many aspects of the fashion industry) often move between, at first, admiration for its new technological possibilities, then disgust and dissatisfaction. The waxing and waning of the popularity of certain fabrics occurs alongside the repeated rebranding, renaming, and revamping of chemically created fibers.

Textiles such as polyester are usually defined in opposition to "natural" fibers: "synthetic fibers—those that do not occur in nature—have been produced since the end of the nineteenth century from both natural and man-made materials."[11] The use of chemically engineered plastic material—the source of both the film strip and synthetic fabric—marks a sharp break from a sole reliance on natural fibers in textile production. Giuliana Bruno says "film can be said to be a form of tailoring. It is stitched together in strands of celluloid, woven into patterns, designed and assembled, now even virtually, like a customized garment."[12] The origin of synthetic textiles is the same as that of filmic material, and the manipulation of the material—the way it is "designed and assembled"—is often similar. Pre-digital film editors handled the film strip by cutting, mending, and patching it in preparation for assembly and eventually projection.

The synthetic material used to make a polyester shirt is noteworthy for its ability to be mass-produced and made accessible to people from a range of income backgrounds. Esther Leslie writes, "when celluloid first appeared, it was used in clothing—corset stays, waterproof shirt collars, cuffs and false shirt fronts." She notes, "at the turn of the century celluloid found application as film strips," and that the cellulose in celluloid was later used in textile manufacturing.[13] The malleability of cellulose-based synthetics made them widely adaptable. Mark Miodownik points out that

> celluloid film was developed by George Eastman as a replacement material for glass plates, and was as central to the photographic revolution as his invention of the compact Kodak cameras. By changing from glass plates to a flexible film of celluloid, which could be rolled up, he made the camera much smaller, lighter, cheaper, and simpler.[14]

Photographic technology has become even more widespread due to the use of individual cellphones. Celluloid, in its photographic and fiber-based forms, widened the scope of twentieth-century consumers.

In its close association with mass production, polyester lacks uniqueness; Lou Taylor writes that "rarity of fibre or cloth type adds exclusivity and high cost and, with those in place, notions of luxury and high positive hierarchical status."[15] In contrast to textiles such as velvet, which I discuss in Chapter 4, polyester does not evoke luxury and rarity. Similarly, early film was considered a "low" art, in part because of its affordability and accessibility for working-class audiences. Polyester's lack of "rarity" is essential to its status as a disparaged textile. Below I follow the different thematic strands of polyester's development through the portrayals of class, gender, and artifice on screen.

Twentieth-century factory production opened up new types of visual culture—including fashion, photography, and cinema—to audiences who were not upper class. The perception of film, especially in the early twentieth century, as associated with "the masses" and therefore not "art," contributed to the idea that widely available media was not worthy of serious study—Walter Benjamin calls this "the same ancient lament that the masses seek distraction whereas art demands concentration from the spectator."[16] Perpetuating this is part of an attempt to define art as class-based. As a result, "bad taste" has taken on a distinct class bias.

We often associate polyester with the tacky men's leisure suits of the 1970s, famously celebrated on screen in the 1977 film *Saturday Night Fever*. *Saturday Night Fever* offers a window into a world where polyester is not embarrassing but covetable. John Travolta's character (Tony Manero) is obsessed with advancing his class standing; in part, this involves upgrading his polyester wardrobe. Tony has achieved respect and admiration in his community for his dancing ability, and his talent gains him some attention outside of his neighborhood. The opening shots of *Saturday Night Fever* introduce us to Tony's Brooklyn environment: tough, crowded, and made of metal and brick. This tells us the rural, natural world will not be an important part of this film; instead, we are in New York City, the center of commerce and fashion in the United States, where characters must negotiate the limitations of their economic place in the city.

Tony has internalized the persistent demand, in fashion, to "keep up" with trends, and he believes this is essential to moving up in class status and out of Brooklyn. Our first look at Tony is a close-up of his shoe—we see him lift his foot up to compare his shoe to a newer, better pair behind glass in a store window. As the initial scene of the film tracks Tony as he walks down the street to his job at a hardware store, he stops at a shop window that displays a shirt he wants to purchase. A conversation with the shop owner reveals that Tony is interested in buying the shirt but he can't afford it. This initial presentation of Tony as longing for what lies out of his reach, embodied in his desire for clothing, carries throughout the film. Both Tony and his love interest Stephanie are obsessed with the visual signs that distinguish them from their working-class surroundings (Tony's passionate commands, "watch the shirt!" and "watch my hair!," exemplify this).

As he prepares for his night out, Tony takes his time choosing the perfect shirt. Shots of Tony reviewing and selecting his shirt are crosscut with scenes from the interior of the disco. The winning shirt is framed dramatically on his bed. Establishing Tony's shirt as central to his presentation of self foreshadows other instances of class struggle and desire in the rest of the film. Stephanie declares a wish to be "refined" (in other words, to separate herself from her provincial Brooklyn surroundings). Tony's longing for the higher-priced polyester shirt shows us that he shares this class aspiration. The shirt, for Tony, is an object of desire that he believes can lead to the fulfillment of another desire: a move up in class status. Tony and Stephanie do not know that the concealment of these aspirations is crucial to convincing others that they are higher class—their unawareness makes them appear comical. Viewers might laugh at their earnest desire to escape their circumstances through superficial objects and mannerisms; similarly, we laugh at the dated presentation of polyester fabric as fashionable.[17]

In the midst of the first nightclub scene, which introduces us to Tony's social circle and establishes the trendy disco aesthetic of the film, the DJ shouts out "I like that polyester look!" to an enthusiastic crowd of dancers. In the world of *Saturday Night Fever*, polyester is fashionable, aspirational, and emblematic of youth culture and style. The primary role of polyester in the film is as a symbol of a general style and attitude. The "look" of the nightclub dance scene in *Saturday Night Fever* is itself influential and evocative of the period in which disco was at the height of its popularity.[18] Specifically, the quality of the lighting captured on camera creates an atmosphere that alternates between tacky and dreamy. The multicolored, blinking lights surrounding the dancers—in the background, overhead, and under their feet—combine, with the soft-focus effect of the lens and smoke machines, to give the scene a warm glow.

In the nightclub setting, the lighting does not try to appear natural; in fact, we are encouraged to admire its fake, plasticky beauty. The multiple light sources bounce off the surfaces of faceted disco balls and synthetic clothing worn by the actors, creating starburst effects and scattered, random dots of light. Polyester fabric takes on a particular sheen under the flashing lights. As Katy Kelleher writes of iridescent fabrics: "Like all iridescent things, it looks best when you can see how light plays over the surface of the cloth. When you freeze it, some of the wonder is lost."[19] The motion of the lights in the

Figure 2.1 John Travolta and Karen Lynn Gorney in *Saturday Night Fever*, 1977. Courtesy Getty Images U.K.

disco, as well as the movement of the dancers and the movement of film itself, create the special look of the disco light in *Saturday Night Fever*.

Saturday Night Fever, a mainstream Hollywood film, makes some reference to changing ideas about conventional masculinity and femininity in the late 1970s. "Stayin' Alive" plays on the soundtrack as we move from Tony's shoes up his body and watch him strutting down the street, eyeing women who pass by. Interestingly, in this film we are encouraged to look at Tony in the same way he looks at women: the camera moves up and down his body admiringly. Not only does this introduce Tony's body as a significant feature of the film—his role as dancer is a major aspect of his character's appeal within the film and the film's success with audiences—but the camera movement feminizes Tony, suggesting we can watch him as a man might watch a woman. This reversal of the male gaze foregrounds the new concept of male femininity that comes up occasionally in *Saturday Night Fever*. Tony's father insultingly compares Tony to a girl, and at one point we see the bullying of gay men and people of color on the streets of Brooklyn. While not explicitly political, the film associates Brooklyn, through Tony's eyes, with outdated ideas about identity expression and femininity. Part of his new "self" is the suggestion that he is considering a more progressive attitude toward cultural difference.[20]

Tony and Stephanie are invested in the idea that fabric and dress are crucial to establishing identity. An important perspective on polyester is a theoretical stance that, particularly in the history of queer culture, celebrates rather than denigrates artifice and plasticity. Artifice, for example in the films of Jack Smith and Kenneth Anger, who I discuss in Chapter 5, is a source of joy and beauty. The ability of plastics to transform and morph into new forms has an enchanting quality. Writing in the 1970s, Roland Barthes admires the "magic" of plastic: "the quick-change artistry of plastic is absolute: it can become buckets as well as jewels." For Barthes, plastic's association with the domestic middle class is part of its extraordinariness:

> until now imitation materials have always indicated pretension, they belonged to the world of appearances, not to that of actual use; they aimed at reproducing cheaply the rarest substances, diamonds, silk, feathers, furs, silver, all the luxurious brilliance of the world. Plastic has climbed down, it is a household material. It is the first magical substance which consents to be prosaic.[21]

The material of plastic—and polyester—has "magical" transformative possibility, not only in the creation of new products but in the creation of self.

Thinking about plasticity as a theoretical concept carries over into discussions of gender and language. Jack Halberstam embraces the political potential in recent debates about pronoun usage and trans identity. Gender transitioning is an ongoing, "plastic" process, not a singular event with a clear beginning and end; in keeping with this attitude, Halberstam states a desire "not to clarify what must categorically remain murky."[22] Insisting on linguistic uncertainty rejects strict definitions of "male" and "female." In refusing to commit to certain definitions, Halberstam retains the plasticity and potential for change in the rhetoric of gender.

Part of the transformative possibility in plastic/synthetic material is in the way it forces us to question the idea of what is "natural."[23] Much of the past and current debates around dress and identity expression return repeatedly to an attempt to define the "natural" and the "unnatural." Textiles in particular are divided into these categories for consumers, even though the processes of textile development and production are often less well-defined, as they incorporate both factory made and naturally sourced materials. "Unnatural" usually refers to the presence of chemistry or chemical processing. In Chapter 3's discussion of the film *Black Girl* I discuss how the Senegalese black woman at the heart of the story gradually restores her natural (not chemically processed) hair as she faces the truth of her situation—she is trapped in the horrors of racism and colonialism. The embrace of natural hair is political and self-affirming; Malcolm X writes of the "self-degradation" of chemically processing his hair, "literally burning my flesh to have it look like a white man's hair."[24] This shows how the term "natural" can assume different ethical connotations depending on viewpoint and cultural context. The word "unnatural" as applied to sexual identities not labeled "heterosexual" has historically been used as a statement of judgment, suggesting an individual is distanced from their natural/"true" self.

As a defiantly unnatural fabric, polyester is uniquely poised to challenge the idea that "naturalness" is superior. Examples in queer history of embracing what is considered "unnatural" include nineteenth-century aesthetes and dandies and Joris-Karl's 1884 novel *Against Nature*. In bodily and architectural adornment, a taste for excessive, maximalist décor has historically been associated with femininity, flamboyance, and dandyism. This aesthetic can be traced further to the world of film melodrama and to layered, heavily ornamented sets and costuming.[25] Synthetic fabric, and especially polyester, is part of an aesthetic tradition that uplifts the excessively feminine and the obviously artificial. Speaking about aesthetic conflict during the mid-1960s to mid-1970s, Mike Kelley explains the use of "displays of femininity as a sign of resistance": he says, "if the female is Other, then the homosexual is doubly Other since he is 'unnatural.'"[26]

The Gay Rights Movement took place alongside other movements such as back-to-the-land, the 1970s craft revival, and a growing awareness of the benefits of organic farming—in other words, a growing popularity of artisanal, anti-chemical, pro-local politics. At this same time, filmmaker John Waters wrote and directed films that celebrated the unnatural, the synthetic, and the artificial. Unlike *Saturday Night Fever*, which was created in the traditional Hollywood film system, Waters's films during this period were outside the industry, and were aligned with the punk, hippie, and other counterculture movements of the time. Waters, who is known for his celebration of uncomfortable subject matter, complicates our understanding of 1970s counterculture. His 1972 film *Pink Flamingoes*, like his 1981 film *Polyester*, takes as its title a tacky object representing 1950s suburbia and middle-class aspiration.

Polyester revels in what society rejects as gauche and repellent, including: unconventional beauty and gender expression, the frustrations of the middle-class housewife, and bourgeois aspirations to move up in class status. The film explores the multiple cultural connotations of this often reviled and trivialized fabric. Like the Douglas Sirk melodramas of the 1950s in which bourgeois women suffer under stultifying cultural restraints—and which influenced Waters—*Polyester* combines ironic camp with sincere feeling to deepen Francine's character and emotional complexity. Utilizing sound and, surprisingly, smell, *Polyester* creates a highly stylized environment in order to articulate Francine's social standing and ongoing despair at her condition.

Before introducing us to Francine, the film opens with an homage to past film-screening gimmicks that tried to sell smell experiences to theatrical audiences. A "mad" scientist announces the film will feature "Odorama," an accompanying scratch-and-sniff card to follow with numerical film cues.[27] The smells include "gasoline" and "skunk"; we are warned, "some odors may shock you." Sensory revulsion is established as an important part of the mood and theme of the film. Soon after meeting Francine, we are acquainted with her exceptional sensitivity to smell. She notices the scent of new clothing, and sniffs an air freshener when she needs to relax. Notably, all of the smells in this beginning section of the film are synthetic. The fake floral, chemical aromas of synthetically produced scent are key to understanding Waters's celebration of the unnatural. Francine's

Figure 2.2 Divine as Francine Fishpaw. Credit: *Polyester* (dir. John Waters, 1981), New Line Home Entertainment, Inc.

(unexplained) attentiveness to constructed, scientifically enhanced smells works with other elements to create an overall multisensory "polyester" aesthetic for the film.

The song that opens *Polyester* carries us through a crane shot of the neighborhood and into the house where the drama begins. Tab Hunter croons Francine's name and calls her a "polyester queen." A handheld camera moves through the front door, around the house, and upstairs to our protagonist, Francine, who is getting ready at her dressing table. Surrounded by the paraphernalia of feminine artifice—hair removal products, home fragrance, perfume—we watch Francine as she engages in the private rituals of bodily preparation. She wears a tight-fitting girdle and bra, and checks her underarms for odor. Francine alters her odor in an attempt to cultivate femininity and conventional heterosexual desire.

Sianne Ngai writes, "artists as well as philosophers have demonstrated that desire and disgust are dialectically conjoined."[28] Throughout the film, Francine's desire to be desired is received with disgust. In *Polyester*, the emotions associated with polyester fabric are also associated with the character of Francine. Over and over, we see people repulsed by Francine—by her vulnerability, her naïveté, her willingness to trust despite being consistently rejected and taken advantage of. Echoing many female leads in "women's pictures" and melodramas, Francine is a victim, and the plot follows her repeated humiliations. Like Cabiria in Federico Fellini's 1957 film *Nights of Cabiria* (and Charity in the 1969 musical version, *Sweet Charity*, directed by Bob Fosse), Francine faces tragedy and disappointment despite her relentless hope that things will turn out differently.

Cabiria is a prostitute, and Francine is a middle-class housewife. Both long for respect and attention while those around them laugh at them and take advantage of them. As targets of ridicule, the lives of these characters inspire sympathy in their viewers. Francine's husband and children are depicted insulting her—even Francine's own mother is cruel to her. Waters skirts the line between comedy and melodrama, using exaggeration to make Francine both comic and tragic. She longs for love and faces repeated rejection. Sandra, the woman with whom Francine's husband is having an affair, brags to Francine that she wears clothes made from "the finest of polyester and I didn't pay for them." The thought of polyester as a "fine" fabric is humorous; at the same time, the attentions her husband has given his mistress while disparaging and rejecting Francine exposes yet another layer of Francine's suffering.

Francine aspires to an idyllic marriage and home life. Like Tony in *Saturday Night Fever*, she imagines life and love outside of her current situation. Francine's longing for a conventional middle-class life is mirrored in the character of Cuddles, Francine's best friend and the one person in the film who is genuinely kind to her. Cuddles was Francine's maid until she inherited money and immediately assumed the life of an American woman born into old-money wealth: she plays polo, wants to move to Connecticut, and plans her debutante coming-out party. Both Cuddles and Francine continually expose their lower-class status and their dreams of different lives; however, while Cuddles embraces her fantasy, seemingly immune to humiliation, Francine becomes an increasingly abject object of derision.

In revealing the collective revulsion at Francine—her odor, her body, her embarrassing emotions—Waters conflates Francine with polyester fabric. Creating what we might think of as a humanized, metaphorical representation of polyester in the fictional character of Francine, Waters explores larger questions of difference, rejection, and the subversive potential in playing close attention to overlooked everyday objects. In examining the attempt to find love in the midst of humiliation, Waters—while also relying on parody and satire—foregrounds the experiences of those who feel marginalized. Here, polyester serves as a useful touchstone for reading Francine: while not necessarily a prominent prop in the film, polyester fabric evokes the intangible emotions of being socially rejected and "othered."

Francine is played by Divine, a man in drag; however, in the film as a whole, trans identity is not a primary theme.[29] The point of the film is not that a man is wearing traditionally feminine clothes but that this is a character who is doing all she can to achieve the supposed rewards of being a good woman. As he does not confront the question of gender expression directly, Waters turns the idea that there is a "natural," biologically determined femininity on its head. In focusing on Francine's character rather than the person acting in the role, Waters successfully shifts the thematic focus from the identity of the actor to sexism and anti-femininity. Julia Serano offers a nuanced reading of how the rigid association of femininity with artifice and "unnaturalness" harms all kinds of women. Serano writes, "in a world where femininity is so regularly dismissed, perhaps no form of gendered expression is considered more artificial and more suspect than male and transgender expressions of femininity."[30] In defining the concept of femininity and breaking down its association with fakeness, Serano rejects the idea that femininity is not feminist.

Disgust for what is "natural" and an embracing of what is fake, constructed, and synthetic acknowledges that plastic and plasticity are part of our contemporary reality. The idea that chemical artifice is now part of everyday life is central to Paul B. Preciado's *Testo Junkie: Sex, Drugs, and Biopolitics in the Pharmacopornographic Era*, a creative and theoretical look at the intersection of sexuality, chemistry, and technology. Preciado describes how plastic, "a viscous, semi-rigid material that is waterproof, thermally and electrically resistant, produced by artificial propagation of carbon atoms in long chains of molecules of organic compounds derived from petroleum, and whose burning is highly polluting," became an increasingly significant cultural and technological, as well as environmentally destructive, force in the twentieth century.[31] Polyester is one result of this social, sexual, political phenomenon.

Significantly, Francine's job in *Polyester*, a film made at the end of the 1970s, is that of a housewife. In the 1970s, second-wave feminist movement in the United States and elsewhere questioned the idea that being a domestic wife and mother was a biologically determined role. The Wages for Housework movement, an international network of groups dedicated to activism for caregiving and other forms of reproductive labor, advocated for recognizing housework as work. In "Wages for Housework and Social Reproduction: A Microsyllabus," Arlen Austin, Beth Capper, and Tracey Deutsch tell us, "this movement attunes us to how the devaluation of reproductive work sustains capitalism's racial, sexual, and global hierarchies. It also attests to the ways in which actors on both the right and the left have disregarded, disavowed and rebuffed demands to take social reproduction and carework seriously."[32]

In discussing feminist works that are increasingly attentive to the importance of technology and chemistry in gender/sexual identities, it is useful to revisit representations of femininity during second-wave feminism. The idea of a "natural" femininity was debated in the

1970s, especially in relation to the perception of women as innately suited to being housewives. Second-wave feminist critique of this labor division raised questions about domestic work and social value. As Rozsika Parker writes,

> The conviction that femininity is natural to women (and unnatural in men) is tenacious. It is a crucial aspect of patriarchal ideology, sanctioning a rigid and oppressive division of labour. Thus women active in the upsurge of feminism which began in the 1960s set out to challenge accepted definitions of the innate differences between the sexes, and to provide a new understanding of the creation of femininity.[33]

Parker's book *The Subversive Stitch* continues to be an influential study at the intersection of feminism and textile studies. Parker explains the way textile work has presented women with a simultaneously liberating and restricting occupation: "Historically, through the centuries, it [embroidery] has provided both a weapon of resistance for women and functioned as a source of constraint. It has promoted submission to the norms of feminine obedience and offered both psychological and practical means to independence."[34] Parker's interest in defining what we think is "natural" in terms of gender is relevant to my examination of textiles, particularly in how textile "craft" was both embraced and disparaged during this time period.

The rise of "hobby" crafts in the 1970s gave the fiber arts increased attention and at the same time the popularity of these crafts—and especially their "hobby" status and association with middle-class housewives—gave them a reputation for being a "lesser" art.[35] Elissa Auther takes up some of Parker's ideas to discuss how art-world value reflects and impacts political and social contexts. Auther claims, "the housewife is a key figure in critical considerations of fiber art, where she signifies amateurism and lack of creativity."[36] Similarly, polyester's targeted marketing to housewives and connection to easing gendered domestic labor contributed to its eventual descent into "tastelessness." I see accusations of "amateurism" as parallel to the denigration of the unpaid work of caregiving, cleaning, and other tasks usually linked to women. Both attitudes dismiss artwork/housework as frivolous and without value.[37]

Auther points to macramé as especially evocative of this association of craft, femininity, and labor: "the macramé hobby craze was problematic for the fiber movement because it reinforced assumptions about fiber as a women's medium of 'low' art status."[38] *Polyester* references this 1970s "hobby craze" at its conclusion, when Francine's daughter Lulu takes up macramé as a hobby and, in keeping with John Waters's extreme satirical viewpoint, eventually uses her craft as a murder weapon. Waters's use of macramé—a gentle, easy-to-learn craft connected to a celebration of the handmade and the "healing" power of art-making—is an interesting counterpoint to the fabric of the film's title. While apparently opposed to the industrial, factory-made work of producing synthetic fibers, a handmade craft such as macramé shares with polyester an association with "lower" class tastelessness. Waters manages to integrate both of these spurned, feminized materials into Francine's story of hope and humiliation.

A primary market for the initial marketing of polyester, middle-class housewives have been utilized, on screen, to expose oppressive conventions of gendered domestic labor. Several other films of this period interrogate the image of the housewife, reframing her as victimized, violent, and/or brainwashed. The satirical horror film *The Stepford Wives* (dir. Bryan Forbes, 1975) is known for embodying many of the anxieties that emerged as a result of increasing feminist consciousness. In the film, a group of suburban husbands succeed in reprogramming their wives from ambitious, politically conscious women into compliant, cleaning-obsessed, and sexually available housewives. In addition to critiquing the inhuman horrors of middle-class white suburban life, *The Stepford Wives* poses important questions about historical beliefs regarding the role of women in domestic labor. Specifically, it asks what is "natural" about gender, femininity, power, class status, and traditional domestic life.

Chantal Akerman's 1976 film, *Jeanne Dielman, 23, quai du commerce, 1080 Bruxelles,* also confronts the supposed "naturalness" of the housewife's work by making the space of domestic labor uncanny and disturbing. Though putting *Jeanne Dielman, The Stepford Wives,* and *Polyester* in conversation may make an unlikely grouping, all three investigate the late 1970s/early 1980s perception of the housewife. While these films do not incorporate synthetic fabric specifically in their representations of housewives, they do rely on fearful visions of technology and a focus on the surfaces of the domestic sphere in order to critique the idea that women (usually, middle-class white women) are destined biologically for this role.

Akerman forces us to witness the stifling domestic world of Jeanne Dielman's apartment, where she engages in the (equally tedious) work of cleaning house and turning tricks. Her home is the site of several inhibiting constructions of "natural" gender and power relations. Akerman's camera stares without visual pause or break as Dielman engages in dull, repetitive tasks; in this way, the cinematography works against the image of an idyllic housewife by making us uncomfortable. As Anca Parvulescu writes,

> Viewers are forced to live the ensuing slowness, repetitiveness, and boredom as a function of spectatorship. Hard at work at the tasks of spectatorship, they learn on their own skin (if they do not already know) how it feels to move from the kitchen to the bedroom and back to the kitchen and then back to the bedroom, each time turning the light on and off, seemingly a million times.[39]

Akerman engages the viewer's body in cinematic space, eliminating the pleasure and relief of varied camera movement in order to assert the housewife's monotonous lived experience.

Figure 2.3 Promotional poster for *Jeanne Dielman, 23, quai du commerce, 1080 Bruxelles* (dir. Chantal Akerman, 1975), with Delphine Seyrig. Courtesy Getty Images UK.

This unidealized depiction of domestic work is based on questioning what is real or fake, natural or unnatural. Ivone Margulies speaks of how Akerman uses "extended duration and fixed frame" to create an unnaturally "heightened" focus on "the dishcloth, her apron, the weight of plates, the soup tureen on the dining table."[40] The claustrophobia of the rooms and unrelenting focus upset any possibility that this might be a cozy or comfortable living environment. Often the cinematography and composition steer our eyes toward the cloth-covered surfaces of her rooms, draped in various floral patterns, signifying the stereotypical femininity associated with domestic interiors. The consistently long takes compel us to consider the patterns, shapes, and surfaces of the apartment in relation to each other—it is as if we are imprisoned in a room and have only one direction in which we can look. In this way the viewer is forced to take seriously and examine closely the overlooked objects of daily life.

As suggested earlier, the overlooked, as well as the disgusting, the fake, and the tacky, find expression in images of polyester. The visceral reaction that many people have to synthetic fibers, especially old forms of polyester, is usually some form of revulsion at the fabric's sensation. Polyester's materiality, particularly in its more repellent forms, merges with its social connotations: it is perceived as an unattractive, outdated object. Notably, *Saturday Night Fever* presents characters who see polyester as desirable rather than detestable. In films such as *Polyester*, people and objects ordinarily dismissed as repulsive and/or invisible are given prominence and empathy. Housewife Francine embodies and embraces the emotional reactions evoked by synthetic fabric, offering a critical look at what we believe about taste, femininity, and the "natural." Exploring how the culturally stigmatized and exploited can be represented and refigured on screen presents possibilities for rethinking taste, class, and gender.

Polyester serves a social role, often as a way to distinguish economic status. Stripes on fabric have also been used historically to mark and divide groups of people. Like polyester, striped patterning on textiles does not communicate one message; instead, the fabric's meaning evolves with context. On film, where meaning is removed from everyday life and condensed into art, a repeated, recognizable pattern can convey nonverbal significance and emotional resonance. In the next chapter I look at how stripes on screen, calling up histories of imprisonment and social isolation, are frequently used to express as well as question social humiliation and marginalization.

3

Screen Prints

Striping and Cinematic Language

Changing perceptions of identity and cultural belonging in the mid-late twentieth century, as shown in filmic representations of polyester fabric, also found expression in patterned textiles.[1] Specifically, the presence of stripes and striping on screen communicate the simultaneously restrictive and liberating conditions of identities in flux. In its dramatic contrast and its evocation of imprisonment, black-and-white striping is particularly well-suited to examine cinematic representations of selfhood and community within the contexts of feminist movement, gay liberation, and post-colonial struggle. Striped fabric within a film's mise-en-scène often shows characters negotiating the imprisoning effects of labeling, humiliation, and persecution. In addition, the presence of stripes on screen facilitates the audience's ability to imagine the viewpoint of the imprisoned and others who resist structures of oppression.

While my other examinations of textiles on film consider fabrics as multisensory—primarily visual and tactile and, to a lesser extent, concerned with sound and smell—this chapter is focused exclusively on the visual presentation of striped textiles. This repeated pattern acts as a warning sign, intended to be easily understood from far away. Originating with prisoners' uniforms, as I explore in the following chapter, black-and-white striped fabric operates as a visual alert, communicating that the wearer should not be approached or touched. Thus the fabric reinforces the purpose of the jail cell—to isolate and deprive the prisoner of tactile experience with other people. On film, striping is often used in a less literal way, to suggest emotional or psychological distance, but it retains its suggestion of physical distance. Rather than appropriating the aspects of textiles that create sensory intimacy with film audiences, striping on screen maintains the pattern's cautionary, threatening quality.

Black-and-white contrast—on film screens and woven surfaces—has a dramatic visual effect, as it provides emphasis and directs viewers' eyes and attention. As Michel Pastoureau points out in *The Devil's Cloth: A History of Stripes and Striped Fabric*, "the spectator's eye cannot *not* be drawn to a striped surface."[2] Both in everyday life and on the film screen, this particular patterning—seen in dress, interior design, upholstery, and elsewhere—is used across media to surprise and repel. The bold contrast of black-and-white striped fabric, especially when used as a prison uniform, tells us to maintain social distance. In the case of prisoners, striped fabric takes on a measure of humiliation, as it indicates its wearer must be observed and thought of as dangerous and/or a threat to others. While historically, in systems of incarceration, striping on cloth has been used to differentiate the imprisoned, it has also been re-appropriated on the film screen as an indicator of self-differentiation. Interpretations of textile patterns become altered by media as the textiles change context, move across time and space, and are projected in different environments.[3]

The striking visual effect of alternating bars on the surface of striped fabric communicates criminality as well as the condition of being jailed, literally and figuratively. In the following readings, I examine how film characters navigate aspects of their identities that are "imprisoned" and/or seen as inferior or threatening within their cultural settings. These films, which emerge alongside political and social movements of the middle-late twentieth century, offer ways of re-thinking identity construction. In addition to suggesting imprisonment, the bold contrasting lines of stripes can also be read as portraying separation, exclusion, and binary thinking more broadly. Black-and-white striping is used within the mise-en-scène to comment on and question social structures, reminding us that these characters are moving around and against (often unsaid or invisible) social restrictions. The oldest film I investigate in this chapter, *A Fool There Was* (dir. Frank Powell, 1915), employs the visually distinctive quality of striped fabric to advance a moralizing message about women and marriage. *Black Girl*, *Querelle*, and *Mildred Pierce* were made at different times and in different countries, but all three document and challenge perceptions of class, race, gender, and sexuality in part through the presence of a stark black-and-white color palette.

Stripes are found not only on printed fabrics but on the film screen itself, in the form of partially obstructed light. The striping effect of light moving through window blinds or other light-filtering props is a common technique, especially in films categorized as film noir. Striped lighting on film not only recalls the visual effect of striped patterning, but, for cinematographers, contrasting lines on screen direct the viewer's eye and help develop drama and mood. The high-contrast appearance of black-and-white stripes in a black-and-white cinematography offers a stylized, impactful composition.[4]

The absence of color in black-and-white films contributes to this dramatic effect. Film technology made significant developments with color film in the 1930s, and color film usage by major motion picture companies gradually increased in popularity before becoming the norm in the 1950s. Before the development of color film, cinematographers were forced to be creative with light, darkness, and gray scale. After color film became widespread, the use of black-and-white film became a stylistic choice for filmmakers rather than a technological necessity. The choice of a limited black-and-white color scale was a creative challenge requiring filmmakers to deliberately exploit the potential of the spectrum between darkest black and lightest white. In black-and-white film, shadows and the gradation of tones between black and white are used to create mood, highlight character struggle, and convey dramatic tension. A textile print with bold contrast will reliably stand out against the varied grays on screen.

Juliet Ash's in-depth study of the prison uniform in the context of fashion and cultural histories, *Dress Behind Bars*, is a starting point for understanding how striped fabric absorbs and disseminates social meaning. Ash's book, which focuses on the United States, the United Kingdom, and Australia beginning in the early-mid 1800s, theorizes how the nonverbal communication of striping works within power structures. Though she makes distinctions among these countries in terms of their dress histories, the primary goals of the recognizable prison striped uniform are consistent: to humiliate, mark as different, isolate from society, and indicate ownership by government. The lingering association of black-and-white striped fabric with incarceration may be due in part to the reproduction of the uniform-clad prisoner in Hollywood film imagery. She argues that although the black-and-white striped prison uniform was removed in the early 1900s, "it was to enter the world outside the prison walls as a visible embodiment of the criminal type in early American films."[5]

Ash explains how the American black-and-white striped prison uniform was born out of the "cheapness of the production of simple black-and-white striped cloth," specifically at Newgate Prison in New York. She continues:

> At the same time as striped cloth was fashionable in the early nineteenth century, and was used in luxurious fabrics such as silks and satins for furnishings and clothing, cheap striped cloth could be easily manufactured in the prison environment. In this way technological developments in fabric production and fashionability in wider society ran alongside the introduction of specific markings of punishment and criminal identity. Stripes were thus part of the

development of technological improvements as much as they were linked to the emergence of the modern prison.[6]

Fashionable striped fabric, according to Ash, is inextricably linked to the history of cheap prison labor—a crucial idea that continues to be relevant as we try to reconcile the demands of "fashionability" with the conditions of making and manufacturing clothing. Elaborating historical connections between the "the modern prison" and textile production, Ash's book unearths parallel developments—in pattern, technology, and cultural change—that have had lasting impact. Embedded within the histories of surveillance and incarceration, stripes continue to connote visual and bodily humiliation despite their disappearance from the prison uniform. Film, a technology central to surveillance and the recording of legal evidence, has extended the specific markings of punishment and crime into cinematic interiors and costuming, and into the photographic presentation of light and shadow.

The message of striped material has evolved over time, while retaining some of its original social connotations. In charting striped print through various aesthetic, cultural, and historical frames, my aim, as Caroline Evans writes, is to begin "re-seeing the past through the filter of present concerns, allowing fragments from the past to illuminate the present."[7] Looking closely at "fragments," or selected details, from several twentieth-century films reveals how the presence of striped fabric speaks to more relaxed views of sexuality and the emerging power of women in the workplace. The rise of globally available visual media means that patterns such as striped fabric increasingly communicate meaning across cultural lines.

Speaking about these types of nonverbal messages, Beverly Gordon points out the significance of striping in enforcing the oppression of marginalized groups:

[A] kind of cloth marking used in the Nazi concentration camps was the black-and-white striped prisoner uniform. Broad high-contrast stripes immediately branded the individual as a prisoner, and made him so conspicuous that escape was more difficult. Here, too, the Nazis were adopting a well-established code system, since stripes were long associated in European cultures with loss of freedom.[8]

"Broad high-contrast stripes" are historically resonant with Western and European audiences in part because of their reference to prison uniforms. How might striping expand out from this specific association into more diverse, perhaps more indirect, interpretations? The use of black-and-white stripes to mark an individual as transgressive can also be employed in film to quickly evoke emotion and develop character. I examine how striped imagery loosens from its original meaning and, through the spatial and temporal movement of film, is reframed to give voice to issues of social entrapment.[9]

Senegalese director Ousmane Sembène employs black-and-white striping in *Black Girl* (1966), a film that examines connections among colonialism, immigration, and domestic labor. Sembène uses black-and-white striped patterning to create character, signify flashbacks, and stir emotion in the viewer, working to reveal the dehumanizing effects of colonialization.[10] The film tracks how visual meaning changes as it moves across geographical and temporal lines, marking narrative turns with significant printed textiles. For Sembène, visual effect has both aesthetic and political resonance.[11] Rachael Langford writes,

> For the francophone African film-makers of Ousmane Sembène's generation, cinema was a way of communicating to other Africans meditations on African experiences, both contemporary and historical, which for the first time were not mediated by outside eyes. Thus for Sembène and his contemporaries in francophone African film-making, the cinema presented itself as a forceful

means of communicating African experience in ways which would counter the images propagated by Europeans determining the identity of Africa.[12]

Part of this effort to communicate "meditations on African experiences" to other Africans was to draw on viewers' intimate familiarity with West African textiles—audiences would immediately recognize and understand the subtext of the fabrics worn by the characters. In *Black Girl*, selfhood and experience are mediated through Diouana's clothing and the patterns that distinguish her living spaces.

Langford points out the prison-like quality of the film's cinematography and "the stark black and white oppositions in the décor."[13] It is in the mise-en-scène of *Black Girl*, as well as in changing representations of Diouana's body—in dress, ornament, and physical labor—that we can see how the film counters colonialist imagery.[14] Black/white contrast constantly remind us of the racist strife at the center of the film's drama. *Black Girl* came out in 1966, only six years after Senegal gained independence. Sembène's use of contrast on film conveys the chaotic reality of those working to navigate this transition. In the time leading to her tragic death, increasingly Diouana is seen wearing her hair natural and choosing to clothe herself with the garments featured in the Dakar flashbacks. As her despair grows and her sense of self becomes more defined in opposition to her colonialist employers, she dresses herself in a way that recalls her home.

The narrative cuts between Diouana's present-day life as a servant in Antibes, France, and flashbacks to her home in Dakar, Senegal. The plot transitions between these two locations underline Diouana's emotional turmoil as she tries to negotiate between her life in Dakar and her new role as a domestic worker in France. In addition to the film cuts and the changes in scenery that mark flashbacks, the print

Figure 3.1 Promotional poster for *Black Girl* (dir. Ousmane Sembène, 1966). Courtesy Getty Images UK.

on Diouana's clothing conveys a dramatic graphic switch between past and present.

When we first see Diouana, she disembarks from a boat from Senegal, holding a white purse and wearing a white dress with black polka dots and a white headscarf and jewelry. While polka dots suggest cheerfulness rather than imprisonment, at this point in the film Diouana has not yet become disillusioned with her journey. The polka-dot patterned dress, a noteworthy contrast to the intricately patterned Senegalese fabrics she wears in her hometown, foreshadows the stark black-and-white environment of her new life in France. The effect of the patterned textiles in the costuming of *Black Girl* brings to mind Karen Tranberg Hansen's assertion that "dress readily becomes a flash point of conflicting values, fueling contests in historical encounters, in interactions across class, between gender and generation, and in recent global cultural and economic exchanges."[15] Textiles play an important role in showing struggle and resistance in Diouana's experiences of racism. In Dakar, Diouana's dress is richly colored and patterned, at once differentiating her identity and aligning her with the people in her community. The fabrics worn by individuals in the Dakar scenes depict Dakar as a place where Diouana has a distinct sense of self, a sense of belonging, and freedom to move and dress as she pleases.

As we follow Diouana through her introduction to her new workplace, and then deeper into her thoughts and memories, we see how the jail-like starkness of her surroundings parallels—and contributes to—her internal frustration and despair.[16] As she enters the home of her new employers, the line of the entryway wall divides Diouana from the white married couple who hired her while in Dakar. As the couple embraces in shadow, the right side of the screen shows Diouana standing next to the mask that decorates the white wall of their home. This mask, which Diouana had previously presented to her employers as a gift, proves an important motif in the film,

Figure 3.2 Mbissine Thérèse Diop as Diouana. Credit: *Black Girl* (dir. Ousmane Sembène, 1966), Doomireew Films.

representing the ornamental "African" object divested of humanness and recontextualized within the home of the colonizer. The mask haunts the film as Diouana's ghostly voiceover recounts the story of her growing disillusionment and rage. The divide between black and white is persistent, symbolized visually as Diouana must clean the prison-striped floors of her employers' home before preparing a Senagalese lunch for visitors who insult and degrade her.

While *Black Girl* speaks broadly about globalization, colonialism, and labor, at the same time it speaks specifically to Senegal's history in West African textile trade and the role of textiles in Dakar culture. As Leslie W. Rabine points out, dress in Senegal does not obey a strict divide between "traditional" and "European" clothing. In fact, "these fashions result from a centuries-old history of weaving together influences from many African, European, and Arabic cultures."[17] In *Black Girl*, Sembène pays tribute to the importance of textiles in Dakar daily life, while also

Figure 3.3 Mbissine Thérèse Diop as Diouana. Credit: *Black Girl* (dir. Ousmane Sembène, 1966), Doomireew Films.

using the division between Senagalese and European prints to heighten the emotional impact of Diouana's tragic decline.

In addition to describing personal and political entrapment, bold striped patterning conveys transgressive sexuality and criminalized difference on screen. The condition of being trapped, as Diouana is, extends into other identity categories such as sexuality. As mentioned previously, early Hollywood film was technologically limited to black-and-white film, requiring that filmmakers exploit the possibilities of this restriction. An example of how black-and-white fabric worked with this technology is found in the Theda Bara silent vehicle *A Fool There Was* (1915), which depicts Bara as a femme fatale who seduces men to their destruction. Described as "a psychological drama," the film presents a moralizing tale about what can happen to men who succumb to "evil" women. The main characters (most of whom are not named, contributing to the sense that they are universally familiar archetypes) include the successful married man John Schuyler, his wife and child, and the "vamp" (Bara). Like other silent black-and-white films, *A Fool There Was* relies on strong visual cues to communicate its message. Especially noteworthy is how the seductress is visually marked as "bad" in opposition to Schuyler's wife and child, who are usually shown wearing white to emphasize their innocence.

Bara, first introduced as a "Vampire" with "one of her victims," wears an eye-catching, body-hugging black-and-white striped skirt and a black jacket with a striped lining. There is some gathering at the thighs of the skirt, and the stripes are arranged in a way that draws our eyes along her legs. Clingy, attention-attracting clothing is part of Bara's look in this film and in others, a costume type that consistently presents her as a sexually liberated modern woman. Bara's femme fatale image was built in part by media images of her in provocative clothing. Adam Geczy writes,

> [Theda Bara] was known as 'the vamp' because she specialized in roles of femme fatale (in almost forty feature-length roles between 1915 and 1919) . . . Sadly, most her films are lost, but the film for which she is most famous was *Cleopatra* (1917), which only exists in a miniscule remnant, although numerous images remain intact. In this costly production, Bara was featured in clothing that was deemed suggestive even for her time.[18]

Bara's celebrity was built in part on the scandal of her clothing. When cultural anxieties about sexuality changed, the clinginess of fabric against her skin lost its transgressive quality. Mick LaSalle writes of later responses to *A Fool There Was*:

> The image of the vamp embodies two fantasies, one paranoid, one romantic. The paranoid fantasy is that sex can kill you. The romantic fantasy is that it just might be worth it. But as the social climate of the twenties got more liberal, the atmosphere of danger that the vamp required for her existence had disappeared. The figure of the

Figure 3.4 Theda Bara as a vamp in *A Fool There Was*, 1915. Courtesy Getty Images U.K.

sexual, independent woman might have been controversial, but it was no longer terrifying.[19]

A Fool There Was embodies this pre-1920s "atmosphere of danger." The striped skirt, which appears at the beginning of *A Fool There*

Was, serves as a visual and moral warning to the audience about the potential dangers of the vamp.

In addition to showing that this is a fashionable woman who stands out from the other characters, the skirt introduces the vamp/mistress as someone who—like a prisoner—is a social outcast and should be humiliated. We are immediately shown multiple stories of men who have been "ruined" by this woman—she is someone who we need to shame and who requires a "warning," as she is responsible for leading men out of conventional society and to their demises. The striped skirt that, along with foreboding tales of destroyed lives, communicates the vamp's danger, reappears at the end of the film in the form of high-contrast lighting. Schuyler's alcoholic decline, estrangement from his wife and child, and obsession with the vamp are enhanced by harsh black-and-white lighting. He is depicted several times in darkness, with a stark light on the side of his face. After losing his job and family, shots of Schuyler and "the vamp" behind the poles of a staircase banister conclude the story: they are now "barred in" by their "immoral" actions.

The danger and subversion in sexuality, as communicated through striped cloth, continued after 1915, in Beatnik culture in the 1950s and 1960s, and later in gay male communities of the 1980s and 1990s. Cultural anxiety around sexuality, particularly homosexuality, has resulted in attempts to criminalize those who identify with and participate in taboo subcultures. The striping long associated with prisoners and criminals—resituated within the context of the film screen—has become a pattern associated with "deviant" sexuality, as in *A Fool There Was*. The larger question of visual patterning in everyday dress as it relates to subcultural meaning can be traced through theorist Dick Hebdige's reading of Jean Genet. Hebdige begins his *Subculture: A Meaning of Style* with a reference to Genet's criminalized, police-confiscated tube of Vaseline: Hebdige writes, "the tensions between dominant and subordinate groups can be found reflected in the surfaces of subculture—in the styles made up of mundane objects which have a double meaning."[20] Hebdige is introducing a discussion of punk style in the United Kingdom, but his emphasis on "surfaces" and "mundane objects" is useful in considering how patterned cloth can communicate more than one meaning, and particularly how something seemingly benign can signal sexual transgression as well as solidarity.

Jean Genet is a useful touchpoint to discuss the intersection of sexuality and humiliation—and how striped patterning communicates this dynamic, especially within gay male culture. Writer Wayne Koestenbaum, in his book *Humiliation*, writes of Genet: "I want to make sure you understand the principle he represents: *although humiliation hurts, it is an oblique pathway to transcendence.*"[21] Genet's characters are trapped within systems of power and humiliation, and these systems fuel sexual pleasure. Translated into film, Genet's work also incorporates the visual symbols of humiliation, including striping.

Jean-Paul Gaultier's use of sailor stripes in the 1990s can be read as a response to the AIDS crisis of the late twentieth century, commenting on the association of homosexuality with fear and delinquency. Gautier drew inspiration in part from the Breton shirts (also called the marinière) featured in Rainer Werner Fassbinder's 1982 *Querelle*. The film, based on a novel by Genet, shows the link between striped fabric's association with criminality and its more recent connotation of rebellious sexuality. In a highly stylized mise-en-scène marked by colored lighting and theatrical sets, Fassbinder traces the adventures of sailor Querelle as he moves through a world of Foucaultian violence, repression, power, and sex.

The settings of *Querelle* are noteworthy for their references to the stage. Like a stage set, built forms rise behind the characters to mark change in location (e.g., the ship appears to be manufactured from several large pieces of wood in order to suggest the presence of a ship, but not necessarily to portray it realistically). A voiceover speaks throughout the film as a sort of chorus, pairing with organ music to create a low-toned, heavy-handed narrative. Characters speak in stilted, monotone voices, not trying to disguise the fact that they are reading written dialogue. Strong orange and yellow lights contrast with blue and purple lights, hitting the actors and the sets with dramatic shadowing. Fassbinder's last film, *Querelle* incorporates these theatrical, over-the-top elements in a more extreme way than in the director's previous work. Significantly, *Querelle*'s "unnatural" acting style and excessive mise-en-scène are also found in *Polyester*, a film from the same period (which also takes "deviant" sexuality as its theme) I discuss in Chapter 2. This sort of theatricality gestures back to the legacy of Kenneth Anger's and Douglas Sirk's work and at the same time points toward contemporary and future possibilities for queer cinema.

The presence of striping in the film, alongside these theatrical references, contributes to its anti-naturalism. A key trait in many films that explore sexuality (as I describe in Chapter 2), stylistic choices that steer the viewer away from "the natural" call attention to the film as a constructed reality. Instead of attempting to imitate or document the "real" world—the world in which anti-gay actions and statements were and continue to result in violence and oppression—a style that is deliberately "unreal" can offer a critique of and an alternative to everyday life. In addition to marking *Querelle* as an important film in the cultural history of gay male expression, the use of a high-contrast style places *Querelle* in a cinematic lineage that explores tensions between individual identity and social perception. Black-and-white striping is, in its visual appearance and its association with the history of prisons, an important pattern to incorporate into discussions of power and sexuality.

Querelle and Nono, the bartender at the bar where the sailors congregate after their ship has docked in Brest, engage in a sexual

Figure 3.5 Brad Davis in *Querelle* (dir. Rainer Werner Fassbinder, 1982). Courtesy Getty Images U.K.

relationship marked by alternating states of power and humiliation. Striped fabric helps chart the series of secrets and betrayals that define their interaction. When we are first introduced to Querelle, wearing his sailor shirt on the ship, the camera cuts to Nono's striped jacket in the bar on land. This graphic match links the two characters immediately. When he first has sex with Nono, Querelle is without his usual Breton striped shirt—but the stripes of his signature costuming carry into the scene. A birdcage in the corner, its bars lit from the side, and the lines of the doorways combine to portray Querelle as entrapped and enclosed. The lighting also makes a striped effect, as if the screen is a printed cloth.

Lines and stripes appear periodically in the film, on clothing and in the scenery, often to signify the subjugated status of the sailor. Close, jail cell-like spaces alternate with shots of the artificial landscape, which is so crammed with larger-than-life set pieces it feels crowded and claustrophobic. The characters move in and out of restricted spaces, transitioning between highly regulated repression and subversive sexual relief. The interrelation between seduction and struggle, authority and lawlessness, is evoked by the contrasting lines of the stripe, both in its connotations of imprisonment and in its stark visual effect. *Querelle*'s thematic emphasis on opposition, rivalry, and struggle for power, existing within and outside of gay male sexual liberation, foregrounds the conflicts in sexual identity formation.

Characters negotiating hierarchies of power, gender, and sexuality are also explored through striped patterning in the 1945 film *Mildred Pierce*. In this film noir, stripes extend from dress and interior fabrics to cinematographic elements of light and shadow—architectural structures in particular take on thematic and visual importance. After her divorce, Mildred must work to feed and provide shelter for her two daughters, and many of her efforts to survive include the selling and purchasing of properties in order to stay afloat. Ownership of houses and the buildings in her restaurant chain are crucial to Mildred's transition from housewife and part-time baker into powerful entrepreneur. Her higher financial status inspires those she loves to manipulate and betray her, resulting in dramatic narrative developments. Throughout the film, background architectural elements display the stark contrast of black and white lines. These stripes create spatial depth on the flat film screen and tell us whether characters are (emotionally, socially, financially) trapped or liberated—or moving between freedom and imprisonment.

At first Mildred is shown in the house she shares with her husband Bert and two daughters Veda and Kay. The fraught relationship between Mildred and her daughter Veda provides most of the film's tension. When Bert leaves to be with another woman, Veda suggests that her mother marry his colleague so they can get a new, better house. Veda conflates her mother with their current home; namely, she finds them both embarrassingly bourgeois. Mildred asks Veda if having a new house means more to her than her mother, and we are left understanding that yes, Veda cares more about having a house that she does not consider shameful. While the film's establishing scenes are generally well-lit, small details such as the contrasting light on Veda as she plays piano and Mildred's striped robe suggest the gradually darkening mood. The dynamic between Mildred and her daughter—primarily, Veda's desire for a life of leisure, and her embarrassment at Mildred's laboring to provide this life—results in the film's most emotionally fraught moments.

Veda's cruelty to her mother and Mildred's humiliation are articulated through stark cinematographic effects. Many film noir films employ low-key lighting, a cinematographic choice which "opposes light and dark, hiding faces, rooms, urban landscapes—and, by extension, motivations and true character—in shadow and darkness."[22] Darkness and shadows hide truths and stark lighting indicate shocking revelations. As Mildred acquires more money, the various buildings she purchases often reveal a background of intersecting lines behind the characters' bodies in action. These nets of light and shadow portray Mildred as increasingly trapped in her position as a midcentury American woman business owner.

Another important feature of film noir is the character of the femme fatale, a dangerous woman (like Theda Bara's "vamp") around whom much of the chaos and drama unfolds. Referencing the women in noir films, Stella Bruzzi states that one of the central symbols of the femme fatale is "a limited, clearly demarcated register of clothes, based on the contrast of light and dark (in keeping with the chiaroscuro mise-en-scène but also indicative of duplicity)."[23] In *Mildred Pierce*, Veda plays the role of the femme fatale, and her "duplicity" is signified in part with striping effects. For example, at the beginning of the film, when Veda is still a child, she expresses distaste for her mother against a wall of lined shadows. When, at the end of the film, Mildred learns of Veda's betrayals, Mildred is literally "in

Figure 3.6 Joan Crawford and Ann Blyth in *Mildred Pierce*, 1945. Courtesy Getty Images U.K.

the dark" about Veda's manipulations until strong lighting clarifies the truth about her daughter.

While dramatic low-key lighting is a well-known component of the genre, *Mildred Pierce* is unusual among noir films for its use of a strong woman protagonist. The bold use of striped patterns in the film helps establish Mildred as a rule-breaking entrepreneur who finds herself in struggle with herself, her family, and society. Print and pattern work alongside other elements to propel and complicate this aspect of the narrative. As Mildred is constantly trying to secure intimate relationships with those around her, the use of striping delineates who is trustworthy and who is (literally) a shadowy character.

Mildred's second husband Monte is introduced to us (and to Mildred) at his beach house, the site of his seduction of Mildred as well as the site of his downfall. He appears in silhouette from behind a wall and door made of long vertical bars. Behind him,

Figure 3.7 Zachary Scott and Ann Blyth in *Mildred Pierce*, 1945. Courtesy Getty Images UK.

reflected sunlight from the window blinds creates the illusion that he is emerging from a caged or jailed space. On the flat screen, the presence of intersecting, variously sized lines create a sense of spatial depth. Thematically, this imprisoning effect suggests Monte's mysterious background as well as the trappings of his desperate financial situation, which he hopes to escape by marrying Mildred. Later, he is aligned with Veda when he too conflates Mildred with her restaurant property, saying he is interested in looking at Mildred, not his "investment." For Monte and Veda, Mildred is an investment: they pretend to care for her so that she will buy their leisure. The constant renegotiating of striping in the film heightens our anxiety as viewers. Who is going to go to jail? Who is trapped? Who is living freely?

After moving up in economic status, Mildred is shown several times working in the office adjacent to her first restaurant. Often accompanied by her former mentor and now employee Ida, Mildred uses her office as a space in which she can both wield her new power and expose her vulnerability. It is in her office that she reveals the particular struggle of how her newfound power and money have impacted her relationships with men. Significantly, Ida, who is identified as masculine and distrustful of men, often joins Mildred in this space. Ida's character is primarily a sounding-board for Mildred's problems negotiating men and money, and Ida—who no longer has management responsibilities and does not appear to be a mother or spouse—is depicted as free from these restraints.

Mildred's restaurant chain is a business dominated by women— it is woman-run, and women perform most of the restaurant labor. Mildred's office is closed off from the restaurant with glass-paned doors, so that the dialogue in the room is kept private but we can see the main dining room bustling outside. This space is both liberating

Figure 3.8 Zachary Scott, Ann Blyth, and Joan Crawford in Mildred's office. *Mildred Pierce*, 1945. Courtesy Getty Images U.K.

(because Mildred can voice her concerns privately here) and restrictive. Similarly, Mildred's role as a powerful businesswoman is imprisoning at the same time as it gives her financial independence. Robert Corber describes Mildred's entrapment in terms of her alternating between traditionally feminine and masculine clothing: "Mildred retains her ability to perform heterosexual femininity, and she alternates between normative and non-normative gender identities even after her rise to success."[24] This "alternating" is also evident in the space of Mildred's office. In this scene, Mildred wears pinstriped suiting fabric and Ida wears a windowpane print. The lines on their garments merge with the lines of the actual windowpanes, the striped wallpaper, the striped blinds, and the striped light on the walls to create a cobweb effect: these women appear caught in the layered, intersecting contradictions of their lives. In this way, the lines and patterns of the mise-en-scène encourage a reading of the characters that takes into account their struggle against and within the constraints of their identities and social positions.

While *Mildred Pierce* offers a complex look at white women, work and power, women of color are not included in this conversation. The character of Lottie, an African American employee at Mildred's restaurant played by Butterfly McQueen, is shown working alongside Mildred and is clearly an important contributor to Mildred's success. However, in a film narrative that prioritizes the seriousness of Mildred's labor, Lottie is presented as trivial. She is to be laughed at, not admired for her labor and struggle, and is not given any depth of character. Lottie is not included in the complex depiction of emotional and societal entrapment that Mildred must negotiate. Though not shown in relation to the various forms of striped patterning in the film sets and costuming, Lottie's invisibility, read through a contemporary lens, is the most stark illustration of imprisonment in the film.

In *Mildred Pierce*, contrasting lines, as in striped fabric and in black-and-white cinematographic effects, work repeatedly to expand

Figure 3.9 Eve Arden as Ida and Joan Crawford as Mildred, in Mildred's office. Credit: *Mildred Pierce* (dir. Michael Curtiz, 1945), Warner Bros.

and extend the film's themes and emotional dramas. The films discussed in this chapter incorporate stripes and striped surfaces to show us the experiences of characters trapped by their desires. Images of psychological and physical imprisonment imply an inability to touch and/or access other people—characters are marked as spatially isolated and disconnected, banned from contact. We watch as Diouana in *Black Girl*, John in *A Fool There Was*, Querelle, and Mildred become increasingly separated from their communities, resulting in psychological distress. They must negotiate love, sexuality, and relationships within unfamiliar worlds of pleasure, pain, and power.

When, as in *Querelle*, sexual and gender identities are figured as criminal, the act of touching takes on a deviant quality. In the next chapter I explore violence and transgression through the specific lens of the tactile. Appearing on screen as fetish and as prohibitive screens, scrims, wall coverings, and clothing, textiles give audiences a more layered experience of the dark desires hidden within obstructed, thwarted, and/or criminal touching. The use of curtains as objects that allow and/or block audience knowledge contributes to the development of cinematic suspense. As we move with the characters through forbidden spaces, we find ourselves implicated in their crimes and entrapped within their longings.

4

Watching Is Touching

On-Screen Transgressions

Before television and digital technologies brought film inside private spaces such as homes, spectators viewed films in environments inspired by the architectural interiors of dramatic theater. Theater interiors delineate the space of the actors from the space of the audience: the theatrical fourth wall prohibits the groups of viewers, physically separated from the stage, from interacting with the performers. A dramatic stage offers some potential for tenuous bodily contact—an actor sneezing, falling, or forgetting a line reminds us they are human; blowing wind, smoke, or fog from an onstage machine may find contact with our skin—while the screen does not contain this possibility.[1] Audiences view the cinematic screen, like a museum display, at a remove. Viewers are restricted from touching paintings and sculpture (we risk destroying the art objects with our touch), just as we are forbidden from touching the film screen.[2]

Unlike painting and sculpture, film and video present audiences with multiple sensory experiences: we both see and hear what is happening on the screen. In addition to sound and vision, fabric can be used to give a sense of tactility to the "forbidden" screen. Textiles, closely associated with physical sensation against the skin, invigorate the screen with the risks posed by the presence of human bodies. This risk is crucial to developing a feeling of intimacy between the viewer and the film. As textiles are intrinsically concerned with touch, they enhance the flat screen with dimension and the promise of tactile sensation. Because we are familiar with the feel of certain fabrics, when we see these fabrics on screen, we can imagine what it would be like to feel them. Just as drapery gives a sense of movement to what might be an otherwise two-dimensional painting or static sculpture, fabric brings to film, already invested with motion, a gesture of physical connectivity with its viewer.

A longing for something unattainable is often expressed on screen by the image of a character gazing wistfully out a window. Though used so frequently it has become a cliché, this image is worth revisiting for its part in articulating restricted touch. The relationship between actor and window can be thought of as paralleling the unrequited relationship between viewer and screen. Like the actor gazing out a window, film audiences look into another world, one that is visually available to us but from which we are blocked—by glass or screen—from touch.

In recreating the frustrated condition of the filmgoer, this cinematic trope encourages us to identify and take on the emotions expressed by the character on screen. Filmmaking techniques that align us with a particular character's point-of-view strengthen this identification. Jennifer Barker explains how the eye and the camera lens merge to enact a sort of "touching": "the viewer caresses by moving the eyes along an image softly and fondly, without a particular destination, but the film might perform the same caressing touch through a smoothly tracking camera movement, slow-motion, soft-focus cinematography, or an editing style dominated by lap dissolves."[3] Barker argues effectively for a new way of seeing, one that takes into account how film machinery works to approximate the sensation of human touch. Our tactile memory of textiles works alongside the mechanics of filmmaking to heighten the feelings associated with an imagined physical relationship.

The films I discuss in this chapter investigate issues around seeing, memory, and social restriction. From milder taboo topics such as infidelity and sex outside of marriage (as in *In the Mood for Love* and *It Happened One Night*) to depictions of violence and crime (as in *Blue Velvet* and *Pickpocket*), textiles blur lines between private and public and confuse the boundaries between cultural norms and societal underworlds. The audience plays an active, immersive role in watching these films, merging multiple senses in order to achieve tactile experience. In her examination of how Gilles Deleuze and Michel Serres's work intervenes with the materiality of cloth, textile scholar Pennina Barnett writes, "the eye, one sense-organ amongst others, does not simply look. It also feels. Its response is both visual *and* tactile."[4] Barnett's "feeling eye" recalls the idea that cinematic representation of tactility is always mediated through the visual. We must rely on our haptic memory to experience this dual sense: looking/feeling.

A useful example of how cloth in film intervenes in a discussion of the haptic is Robert Bresson's 1959 film *Pickpocket*. *Pickpocket* deals with criminality and transgressive touching through a discussion of spirituality and ethics, in addition to depictions of criminal strategizing. At various points in *Pickpocket*, the camera, often through close-up shots, records the characters as they move through the various steps involved in performing petty crime: working through the mechanics of selecting victims; engaging in the uncomfortable intimacies of touching and then removing items from pockets; and finally fleeing with the desired item. Michel, the film's protagonist, develops an increasingly obsessive interest in the intricacies of theft—including how to fold/unfold papers and fabrics correctly, and how to use touch (not just sight) to determine what is open or closed, revealed or hidden.

The coordination of Michel's fingers and eyes is crucial to his success as a thief. Picking pockets requires that he use his fingers to deftly manipulate fabric, and he must develop an ability to accurately measure distance without visual assistance. Michel's blind seeking and grasping of folded fabric is a sensory reversal of the film viewer's position: unable to physically experience the surface texture projected on the screen, film audiences rely on what is made visible as well as our tactile memory of textiles. While we cannot enter Michel's world, we are encouraged—visually, spatially, and emotionally—to identify with him.

This is evident in a crucial scene at the beginning of *Pickpocket*, when we are securely in Michel's point of view before we even see him in the frame. Michel's voice narrates the scene, reflecting on it from the future. We follow Michel's eye as he studies a woman who transfers money from her purse to place a bet. Her crocodile purse and distinctive large hat serve as markers—we recognize who she is because Michel and the film camera have already focused our attention on her accessories, forcing the viewer to note the significance of these objects. Standing behind the woman as she watches a horse race with a crowd of onlookers, Michel carefully negotiates the theft of the remaining money from her purse. Laura McMahon writes of this scene:

> Intercut with frontal shots of Michel watching the race over the woman's shoulder are four close-up shots of the long fingers of his hand working on the bag: trying the clasp, undoing the clasp, slipping under the flap of the bag, and, finally, the triumphal extraction of the money. These close-ups figure the bag — its initial resistance and then gasp of opening — as a body itself, or as an extension of the woman's body. The hand slipping slowly under the flap of the opening is like a hand feeling its way into folds of clothing or flesh.[5]

As Michel watches the woman and the woman watches the race, we observe Michel as he manipulates the clasp of the purse and successfully removes the bills. The camera pays special attention to the fact that he appears to be looking in the direction of the race while actually his concentration is located in his hands and fingertips. The camera moves back and forth to show how his eyes remain looking forward at the same time as his hand and fingers move separately from his line of vision. This brief sequence maps out, for the audience, how Michel has developed fingers that "see." Others in the crowd could potentially watch Michel's eyes to determine where he was looking; by disconnecting his action from his eyes, Michel engages in a kind of self-blinding in which he can hide his illegal activity.

Sarah Montross speaks of "considering the screen as a bridge between physical and virtual worlds, a tactile membrane, or a device that fosters both exclusion and intimacy."[6] The "tactile membrane" of the screen offers potential for exploring the limits of intimacy and spatial distance, and gives a dimension of touchability to film-watching.[7] Representations of fabric on screen, as well as in films that treat the screen as a type of fabric, heighten the interplay between viewer and projected image. In *Pickpocket* the unstable boundaries around transgressive touching, as shown through close-ups of Michel's developing sensory knowledge of textiles and other materials, encourage the viewer to identify as an observer of his crimes. When the audience member is positioned as a witness in relation to the events on screen, the viewer is implicated in these (fictional) crimes. In David Lynch's 1986 film *Blue Velvet*, the main character, Jeffrey, in a crucial early scene, is a witness to violence. As our viewpoint is Jeffrey's, we too are trapped in the horror of watching criminal violence.

Criminality, visuality, and touch are embodied in the fetish, a central aspect of *Blue Velvet*. In examining the velvet fetish in the film, I first look at the role memory has in developing a tactile screen. Laura Marks's theory of haptic visuality provides a foundation for this concept; as Marks writes, "haptic visuality requires the viewer to work to constitute the image, to bring it forth from latency."[8] Memory is essential in the creation of tactile/visual experience. The "latent" image is summoned in part through tactile memory.

In order to depict multidimensional sexual tension on film, viewers need to engage their memories of sensory experience. Because the screen prevents us from interacting with the filmed fabric in a direct way, we must rely on our remembered understanding of sensation to engage physically with the scene. High-density textiles are of particular interest here. Our tactile experience of materials such as fur and velvet is often memorable. I remember the first time I touched real fur: I was a child and sitting at a performance in a large concert hall in San Francisco. The woman next to me had draped her fur coat over the back of her seat, and some of it fell onto my seat. I allowed myself to touch it a few times throughout the performance, indulging in its unfamiliar softness.

Fur, a material prized for its density and touchability, has long been linked to fetishism. In his classic novel of sadomasochism, *Venus in Furs*, Leopold von Sacher-Masoch places fur at the center of his image of the cruel object of obsession. His narrator, Severin, tells his beloved that fur "exerts a strong and mysterious physical attraction to which no one is immune."[9] Freud also speaks of the fetish in relation to hair: "what is substituted for the sexual object is some part of the body (such as the foot or hair) which is in general very inappropriate for sexual purposes, or some inanimate object which bears an assignable relation to the person whom it replaces and preferably to that person's sexuality (e.g. a piece of clothing or underlinen)."[10] Freud uses the example of hair and Sacher-Masoch references fur in order to illustrate the sexualized "inanimate object." Interestingly, the examples of fetishism they select both possess the dense tactile surface of animal/human skin.

Walter Benjamin's definition of the fetish calls attention to the blurred distinction between "organic" and "inorganic": "in fetishism, sex does away with the boundaries separating the organic world from the inorganic. Clothing and jewelry are its allies. It is as much at home with what is dead as it is with living flesh."[11] For Benjamin, the fetish animates the dead and/or inhuman. Ulrich Lehmann, looking at Benjamin, Freud, and Marx on fetishism, explains, "the sartorial product itself is extremely close to its wearer—a second skin—but as a commodity, not to mention an artificial status symbol, essentially estranged from him or her. It maintains a distinct meaning and value of its own. Therefore it has an additional potential to become a fetish."[12] The simultaneous intimacy and distance of the fetish is central to velvet's role in *Blue Velvet*. Like animal fur, velvet is touchable, luxurious, and both skin-like and "estranged." In the film, Frank Booth, a character who animates and fetishizes blue velvet, gives intense power to fabric while treating humans like unfeeling objects.

Like fur, velvet is a dense-pile fabric associated with economic luxury and physical sensation. Historically, velvet has been linked to royalty, tapestries, and religious garments—as a costly fabric, it was for a long time accessible only to the upper classes. Velvet is a pile weave, meaning the surface is raised and has a short, densely woven surface. Dense-pile fabrics have a unique relationship to touch. Unlike the skin-like smoothness of satin, velvet contains the texture and softness of hair. It moves and responds to pressure, giving it an ever-changing quality. The composition of velvet impacts the look of the textile; as Alexandra Shulman writes, "black cotton will never look the same colour as black velvet."[13] A feature of velvet is the visibility of its texture, which increases the intensity of its color: "cut pile, as in velvet, reveals the density of color in the cut cross-section of the tightly packed dyed yarn."[14] Velvet's intense, dynamic color and texture give it a strong sense of touchability, which is crucial to its status as fetish in the previously mentioned film *Blue Velvet*.[15]

Titling the film *Blue Velvet* immediately highlights the role of blue velvet as prop, concept, and symbol in the film. Surprisingly, few

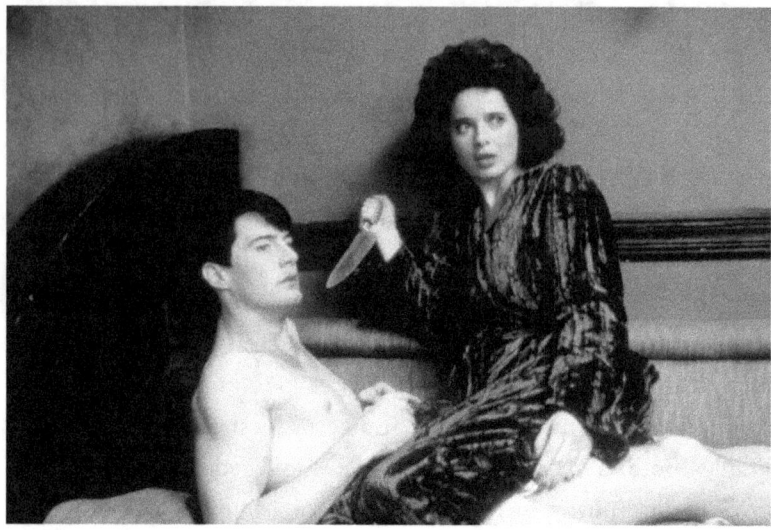

Figure 4.1 Kyle MacLachlan and Isabella Rossellini (wearing a blue velvet robe) in *Blue Velvet*, 1986. Courtesy Getty Images UK.

critics have given sustained examination to the role of velvet in the film. The primary interest in velvet has been in regards to its status as a fetish object. Charles Drazin observes that "if Frank associates the blue velvet with many, often contradictory things, perhaps finally it stands best as a symbol for inexplicable, ever-shifting infatuation."[16] I am interested in how, in addition to and in connection with the fetish, velvet fabric in particular materializes desire in a way that reverberates for the audience.[17] The unstable, malleable quality of the fetish—and of velvet fabric—contributes to the film's sense of anxious uncertainty.

Part of the definition of fetish is that it materializes desire. The fetish object is imbued with desire, and touching the object is the taboo that the fetishist longs to transgress. *Blue Velvet* intricately—and terrifyingly—links taboo and tactility on screen. The textile of the title operates within the film's plot as prop, both in clothing and in pieces of the fabric, and in the film's use of the popular song "Blue Velvet." We see Dorothy Vallens wearing a blue velvet dress; we also watch

Frank as he caresses scraps of blue velvet fabric.[18] Throughout, blue velvet holds Frank's anxieties and desires, concealing the unspoken source of his violence and criminality. Dorothy, who wears blue velvet and sings "Blue Velvet," is the primary victim of his violence. He longs for her and wants to control her; at the end of the film, she appears naked: free of blue velvet and free of his oppressive infatuation.

Throughout the film, Frank is desperate to possess the inaccessible object of desire that lies within and beyond blue velvet (and Dorothy). The exact nature of this object, and the reason for the fierceness and violence of his longing, is never revealed to us. Robert Stoller tells us that "a fetish is a story masquerading as an object"—but in *Blue Velvet*, the "story" of Frank's behavior is never explained.[19] Unlike other films that present us with the trauma motivating violent impulses, *Blue Velvet* refuses to give the audience a reason for Frank's criminal impulses. *Blue Velvet* does not explain his fetish through a confessional moment or revelatory flashback that would give us a psychological reason for his violence. The absence of logic in the film, particularly in regards to Frank, is crucial to creating the dreamlike mood and moments of nightmarish horror.

Diverging from the Freudian attitude, which explains psychosis via the revelation of childhood trauma, Lynch immerses us in the specific terror of not comprehending why violent, unreasonable acts happen. In "Freud, Fabric, Fetish," Anne Hamlyn describes the creation of the fetishized object; for Freud, Hamlyn argues: "the fetishist goes back to the moment just before, or the moment after, the traumatic encounter and fills in the absence artificially with a reassuring image—an image that will later become the basis for the fetish object."[20] Frank's "reassuring image" is blue velvet, and his—and our—relationship with it is visual and tactile, not based in any conscious awareness of a specific "traumatic event." As film viewers, we are often encouraged to engage in what Hamlyn calls a "sensuous voyeurism," in which we engage emotionally with the "nonverbal (optical, oral, tactile) elements of the *mise-en-scène*."²¹ The significant presence of blue velvet in the film compels Lynch's audience to assume the role of the fetishist in addition to that of the voyeur/witness.

In *Blue Velvet* the audience most noticeably identifies with the protagonist Jeffrey as he moves through the plot development and, strikingly, when he is witness to Frank's violent assault on Dorothy in her apartment—our point-of-view is his, and we experience shock and repulsion along with his character, who is as passive and unable to act as the film audience. This moment of voyeurism in the film is different from the "sensuous voyeurism" we might enjoy while observing alluring, touchable fabrics in a film's mise-en-scène. A pleasurable haptic visual sensation is, in *Blue Velvet*, more associated with the fetishist's (Frank's) perspective. When, in this film, we take pleasure in the way the camera admiringly focuses and lingers closely to richly textured surfaces, we take on the position of fetishist. We move through different character perspectives, never completely understanding Frank's initial "traumatic encounter" and why he soothes his trauma with blue velvet. For Frank, the fetishist textile is what blocks his trauma; for the characters and for the film audience, this instability and the lack of knowledge about his trauma is what creates what Hamlyn calls "an intolerable anxiety."²²

Frank's particular unstable sense of reality can be traced through the use of music in the film. He lip-syncs along with sentimental pop ballads, offering a window into his emotional life. The lyrics of the songs, like literal blue velvet fabric, provide Frank with a realm of safety. Lip-syncing in particular emphasizes the performer's identification with the song lyrics. We see Frank lip-sync to "Blue Velvet" and to "In Dreams." Alice Kuzniar describes the "In Dreams" scene as "inverted ventriloquism, where the living person acts as the dummy whose voice comes from elsewhere." This technique "encapsulates the problem that the film illustrates, that is, the disjunction of sound from image, hearing from seeing, voice from body."²³ This disjunction also describes Frank's velvet fetish. For Frank, velvet is estranged from Dorothy, and it is the textile, not the person, who "speaks" to him.

The song "Blue Velvet," which we hear several times over the course of the film, visually and lyrically articulates Frank's longing. The song describes the speaker's loss of a woman who wore blue velvet, and how the narrator "still can see blue velvet/through my tears." The woman is gone, but the speaker has a vivid recollection of and attachment to the fabric she wore. "In Dreams," the other song featured in the film as a link to Frank's obsession, is another depiction of a narrator who visits a lost love in their dream life. The camera pays careful attention to Frank's face while these songs play: he is emotional, needy, and clearly identifying deeply with the lyrics as he mouths the words he has memorized. Frank, in a state of frustrated desire, seeks the tangibility of blue velvet. He takes the song lyrics literally, believing that he can access the lost beloved through other means—specifically, through touching blue velvet fabric. It is the tactility of the velvet that he seeks as relief from his intangible and uncontrollable feelings. Blue velvet is a dangerous fetish, as it shows us Frank's inability to distinguish between fantasy and reality.

When we watch Frank listen to the song "Blue Velvet," we see him in a state of sentimental longing. Touching scraps of blue velvet seems to offer him access to this calmer mental state—it works as an infantile form of comfort for him, and also materializes and makes manageable his out-of-control emotions. In the disturbing rape scene in Dorothy's apartment, Frank holds a scrap of blue velvet in his mouth in a manner similar to a baby holding a transitional object. Closer to the end of the film, Frank returns to another crime scene in the apartment—he is there to take back the blue velvet gag from a dead body and get Dorothy's blue velvet robe from the bedroom. These bits of fabric have more meaning for Frank than human life. Blue velvet is, for Frank, a way to access the thing (security? love? his mother?) he longs for most. In the nightclub where we see Dorothy perform "Blue Velvet," Jeffrey, unnoticed by Frank, studies Frank as he caresses a piece of blue velvet. Through Jeffrey's eyes, we take note of Frank's unusual behavior. While both men are obsessed with Dorothy, Frank's simultaneous obsession with blue velvet estranges and vilifies his character.

An essential part of blue velvet's status as Frank's fetish is his need to hold it and his compulsion to touch it. Much of *Blue Velvet* is concerned with intimacy and closeness, both literally and figuratively. Jeffrey's growing physical and emotional proximity to his hometown's criminal underworld is what makes the film suspenseful. Early in the film, a sequence in which the camera descends underneath a suburban lawn into the seething insects and mud below—as we listen to "Blue Velvet" on the soundtrack—indicates that the camera will be delving into issues of nearness and distance (as well as disgust and horror). The threat to Jeffrey grows as he leaves his familiar neighborhood surroundings and moves farther away to the outskirts of town. Over the course of the film, Jeffrey gets closer and closer to the town's shadowy underworld, culminating in the arrival of Dorothy at Jeffrey's house at the end of the film. At this point, Jeffrey's secret life is exposed and the line between the two worlds is transgressed. As Paul Whittaker and Clio Padovani write of this moment in the film: "when [Dorothy's] presence is detected it disorientates the scene completely."[24] Jeffrey's initial distance and separation from Dorothy and Frank has been erased, and this broach unnerves the seemingly quiet small town community.

Similarly, the role of blue velvet in the film becomes increasingly sinister. In Jeffrey's first encounter with Frank, Dorothy's blue velvet robe plays a crucial part in introducing Jeffrey to Frank and Frank's demand for physical control. Frank finds Jeffrey in Dorothy's apartment and takes him out to his car for a "ride." During the ride Frank frightens and intimidates Jeffrey (and the audience). Before leaving Dorothy's apartment, Frank commands her to put on her blue velvet robe. After pulling over the car and bringing Jeffrey outside to threaten him further, Frank first presses a piece of blue velvet fabric against Jeffrey's cheek, then he and his cronies beat up Jeffrey. Blue velvet transforms, for Frank, from a source of comfort to a weapon-like instrument of intimidation. Though velvet itself is not dangerous, Frank uses it to demonstrate his capacity for violence. He forces physical contact with Jeffrey, and the striking irrationality of using a scrap of velvet as a threat is unnerving.

The association of Frank with scissors, cutting, and with his blue velvet fetish suggests that his role in the film is similar to that of a sewer, or, in cinematic terms, the film editor who cuts and pieces together the material of the film. The film editor is the person in charge of manipulating the existent film into a narrative with a beginning and end. Walter Murch speaks of the "violence" of editing film: "at the instant of the cut, there is a total and instantaneous discontinuity of the field of vision."[25] Following from this logic—that cutting is a kind of violence done to the film strip—in *Blue Velvet*, Frank treats people as if they are film strips, cutting them and threatening to cut them in pieces. Thinking of film editing as a kind of dismembering connects back to the discovery of the severed ear (severed by Frank, we learn later) that initially propels Jeffrey's curiosity and subsequent risk-taking, and therefore the film's larger narrative.

In the early part of the film, Lynch encourages us to conflate the scissors-as-weapon with the film cut. We move abruptly from the detective saying "it looks like the ear was cut off with scissors" to a shot of scissors cutting through the "caution" tape surrounding the place where the severed ear was found. The sound of cutting scissors is also noticeably loud. The layering of the spoken word "scissors," the sound of scissors, and the view of cutting scissors on screen, all while bridging a film cut, create a not-very-subtle link between the scissors used to violently harm the body and the cutting work done by film editors. Here we can see a collapsing of the boundaries between skin, fabric, and film material—all can be cut and manipulated by someone wielding a pair of scissors. On film, a cut marks a place where the editor is limiting the amount of information available to the viewer, creating, as Murch writes, a visual "discontinuity." Thinking of the film editor as someone who controls access and decides what information to hide or reveal shows how Frank's character can be read as an editor/manipulator who brandishes his scissors as a threat.[26]

Scissors operate as a motif, as Frank repeatedly uses them as a weapon to intimidate and harm others throughout the film.[27] David Copenhafer points out that the film's sound design heightens the impact of Frank's scissors: "while scissors themselves may not be the most menacing object, the meaning of the gesture and of the sound becomes apparent when one realizes that he may have cut off the ear of Dorothy's husband with the very same instrument."[28] Frank "signs" his acts of violence with scissors and pieces of blue velvet. When we see him brandishing scissors, we know he is the one who cut the lost ear.

Frank's fetishizing of blue velvet is obsessive and violent, but textiles also carry the potential for articulating tamer feelings of love and desire on film. The role of touch in depicting sexual tension between characters is particularly important. Jennifer Barker describes, in relation to film and the haptic, how a "tactile perception of the world manifests itself in art that emphasizes texture and materiality—the grain of video imagery, for example—and encourages the viewer's gaze to move horizontally over the image, like fingertips caressing a particularly lush fabric or the dry grain of a sandy beach."[29] The haptic eye enjoys the film, "caressing" its "lush fabric." Props on film (such as screens, scrims, and room dividers) as well as obstructive editing techniques (framing, cropping, and cutting) serve to delay or prevent the character/viewer from seeing/touching the desired object. This thwarted gratification heightens our interest.

Some films imagine how audiences might transcend the prohibition on physical contact with the film screen. The condition of frustrated desire—a lost love; an unrequited passion; an unavailable love-object—occasionally manifests as a fantasy of transcending the barrier between audience and screen. The screen marks the transition between a state of desire and the consummation of fantasy.[30] The dual nature of the privacy screen in this context—as a site of covering and also revealing—is important in developing themes of erotic transgression and longing on film.

As Laura Marks writes, "tactile visuality is still not touch."[31] Marks states, "haptic visuality implies a familiarity with the world that the viewer knows through more senses than vision alone. Changes of focus and distance, switches between haptic and optical visual styles, describe the movement between a tactile relationship and a visual one."[32] The unique qualities of on-screen textiles exemplify this idea: watching textiles can be a "tactile" experience, yet it does not allow for actual physical contact. This tension is useful in illustrating the condition of longing on film. Sumptuous fabrics such as velvet are especially evocative as their visual presence sparks tactile memory and experience. This dynamic around touch and the film screen opens up thematic possibilities for depicting desire beyond fetishized criminality and violence.

The topic of longing is central to Wong Kar-Wai's film *In the Mood for Love* (2000), which examines the limits of marital fidelity and unspoken desire via layered, vibrant surfaces. Throughout the film, the screen is saturated with rich textures and bright floral prints. The plot, which focuses on a man and woman whose respective spouses are engaged in a love affair, and who begin to desire each other, explores the nonverbal expression of unrequited love. The ending frame of *In the Mood for Love* shows us the man, looking back on this time and recalling his life as described in the main film narrative as "something he could see, but not touch."[33] An overwhelming array of appealing colors and textures of fabrics—which, as film viewers, we can access only visually—further codes the love-object as untouchable. I agree with Sarah Gilligan, who writes of this film: "through the haptic pleasures of textiles and adornment, the spectator is able to form their own narrative world in which touch and feel plays just as integral a role to the transformation and performance of identity as visual signifiers do."[34] However, I would build on this statement by arguing that the "integral" role played by touch is specifically that of presenting a tactile surface which cannot be accessed, ultimately producing both pleasure and frustration in the viewer.

In the Mood for Love, in its costuming and set design, creates a multisensory, multidimensional environment which enables complex emotional reactions. Mrs. Chan's cheongsam collection is particularly evocative.[35] Liz Rideal says that the cheongsam "and the fabrics that form them punctuate the narrative and change the pace of the film by their color and pattern; rich flower bursts, jazzy geometric designs, or combinations of these."[36] In addition to tracking the development of the characters and the narrative, the fabrics—not just in costuming but on walls and windows—contribute to a deeply intimate emotional experience. Of *In the Mood for Love*, Giuliana Bruno writes, "the story unfolds in interiors. We are always inside, even when we are not."[37] The layered, close surfaces ensure that we remain immersed in the psychological lives of the central characters. Interiors that are perpetually "unfolding" recall the continuity of the "infinite" Baroque fold, through Deleuze: "the problem is not how to finish a fold, but how to continue it, to have it go through the ceiling, how to bring it to infinity."[38] The cheongsams, wallpapers, upholstery, and other fabric coverings in the film build to develop intricate surface depth on the screen, suggesting the infinitely folding and unfolding mysteries of the characters' emotions. I examine this phenomenon further in Chapter 5, in reference to the presentation of intangible feelings associated with moving curtains.

In the Mood for Love shows how textiles express character interiority and longing, and the dynamic between interior and exterior is especially evocative in this film—the surfaces in the film are layered, and the camera's attentiveness to these dense constructions of color, light, and texture infuse them with significance.[39] Another example of how film screens and fabric surfaces work together to navigate issues of desire and privacy in the cinematic space occurs in *It Happened One Night* (1934). In this screwball comedy, spoken desire is embodied in fabric, though its effect is more comical and direct than that of *In the Mood for Love*.

Peter (Clark Gable) and Ellie (Claudette Colbert) are brought into close proximity on a bus, which then brings them into various awkward situations in which they must negotiate distance and physical closeness. Forced to pretend they are married and stay in a cabin together, Peter puts a blanket between his bed and Ellie's bed for privacy. The hanging cloth used as a privacy curtain slices the screen space, creating two semi-private rooms where we can see the characters' reactions to each other. Peter has started to undress in front of her—she is watching him—and she goes to the other side of their makeshift screen. He sees her clothes flung over the curtain to communicate that she is undressing on the other side. They spend the night and morning together platonically, but the presence of the privacy screen heightens the scene's sexual tension and highlights the strict taboo (at the time) against an unmarried couple spending the night in the same hotel room.

The next morning, a wipe across the film screen mirrors the blanket sliding on its rail. At this point in the film, Peter and Ellie outwardly snub each other; however, as audience members, we can see their growing mutual affection and desire to be near each other. The movement of the curtain—and the movement of the wipe across the screen—suggests a potential for open expression of their emotions. The restrictions limiting their intimacy are starting to loosen and relax,

Figure 4.2 Claudette Colbert and Clark Gable in *It Happened One Night*, 1934. Courtesy Getty Images UK.

and it appears they may soon reveal their feelings for each other. Gen Doy writes that drapery "can be perceived as covering something and *at the same time* as revealing, or about to reveal, something."[40] In this scene from *It Happened One Night*, we can see what is on each side of the partition, and can therefore experience the fabric's simultaneous covering/revealing.[41] The film screen and fabric screen work together to reveal the characters' vulnerabilities and create anticipation about their future.

The unique technology of the film screen, which allows for visual intimacy and the suggestion of tactile experience, presents opportunities for filmmakers to examine issues such as fetishism, criminal obsession, and the more mild taboo of sex outside marriage. In the following chapter I continue to explore the voyeuristic thrill of watching/touching what is forbidden in scenes that employ moving fabric in order to create suspense. Curtains, waving skirts, and blowing fabric cover and uncover the screen as they develop mood and character. The novelty of photographic movement has been a central part of film's historical and cultural appeal; as I show, the motion of textiles on the motion picture screen has been an especially effective detail in provoking and engaging the viewer.

5

Moving Pictures

Magic, Suspense, and Textiles in Motion

For silent film audiences, a primary attraction of the new cinematic image was its ability to portray recorded motion, as the technology of the "moving picture" was a novelty at the turn of the twentieth century. In addition to the moving film strip's ability to show motion, the images projected on screen inspired awe for their realism and for the special effects filmmakers achieved with props and costuming. The history of film begins with the recording of movement, and bodies and textiles in motion were a significant part of what was initially represented on screen.

The motion of the camera, and the camera's ability to capture and record motion, works with moving textiles to give form to abstract, hard-to-define feelings. Blowing textiles—curtains, other wall coverings, and dress—animate the mise-en-scène and can be manipulated to suggest various emotional states. Because textiles are intrinsically connected to questions of movement on and around bodies—for example in considering elasticity, drape, and fall—they can enhance mood and explain aspects of film atmosphere and character emotion that may not be understandable through other means.

Advances in photographic motion technology altered how early twentieth-century audiences viewed the world. As Rebecca Solnit writes:

> Motion pictures changed the relationship to time farther; they made it possible to step in the same river twice, to see not just images but

events that had happened in other times and other places, almost to stop living where you were and start living in other places or other times. Movies became a huge industry, became how people envisioned themselves and the world, defined what they desired and what was desirable.[1]

Solnit begins her study with an examination of Eadweard Muybridge's development of motion-study photographic technology, and an analysis of how a new perception of motion, in photography and film, changed our sense of space and time. Those working during the early days of filmmaking learned that they could focus their audience's eyes by not only depicting movement of people and objects, but by using the camera to frame and focus, shaping and editing how viewers see the world of the film. As film grew in popularity, filmmakers began to make decisions about how to reveal or hide visual information. The mechanical tricks of the cinematographer and editor—including the use of cuts, distance, speed, and special lenses, among other techniques—guide our eye, forcing us to pay close attention to certain elements while obscuring other details.[2]

One of the first popular films showed dancer Loie Fuller performing the "serpentine dance"; in this dance, the performer moves wands attached to large draped pieces of fabric to create a flowing, swirling effect. Catherine Hindson explains: "the serpentine dance evolved as a sub-genre of the skirt dance, a form which had a long stage history before it was captured by early filmmakers. It became, arguably, the biggest entertainment craze of the 1890s and the close of the century saw its popularity peak."[3] This theatrical "craze" coincided with the beginnings of film, and several versions of the recorded dance were shown to cinema audiences in the mid-1890s. Many of the earliest films incorporated popular performance to increase numbers of viewers and at the same time expose more people to the new motion technology.

The filmed serpentine dances are noteworthy for the way the camera captures light and motion on the wing-like fabric. In addition to showing early film's novelty of movement, images of blowing fabric on film became an effective way to establish the environmental and, as mentioned earlier, emotional atmosphere of a scene.[4] For example, in *Singin' in the Rain* (1952, dir. Stanley Donen), an important dance sequence incorporates moving white fabric to articulate the sexual tension between two dancers. The textile swaying between and around them gives a physical and visual dynamic to their emotions. Liz Rideal says of this scene in *Singin' in the Rain*: "[the two characters'] electric attraction is heightened by the tensions displayed in the erotic movement of the white cloth that envelopes [sic], ruffles, tangles, distances, binds, and bonds them together. The length of cloth suggests the pure white linen of a bedroom storm while simultaneously and coyly avoiding this."[5]

In order to investigate more deeply the way textiles in motion on screen can voice that which cannot or "should" not be spoken,

Figure 5.1 Cyd Charisse and Gene Kelly in *Singin' in the Rain*, 1952. Courtesy Getty Images UK.

I look at several films from the United States, the United Kingdom, and France from the 1940s. During and after the Second World War, the film industry enjoyed prosperity and popularity. Not unlike the role of Hollywood during the Depression Era of the 1930s, as I discuss in Chapter 1, films in the 1940s offered audiences an affordable, accessible escape from a reality that for many was violent and uncertain. Before the widespread use of television in the 1950s, film theaters were generally easy to find and crowded with people from all class backgrounds. The cinema provided a space for the collective processing of tragedy and unrest, and the screen reflected these difficult emotions. In addition, during the 1940s the Hayes code placed restrictions on what could not be shown on film, so filmmakers were forced to communicate taboo topics through other, more indirect, means.

These factors—the incomprehensibility of war and the suppression of "transgressive" behavior—underlined a need for effective nonverbal expression on film. Specifically, textiles in motion on screen give tangible, visual form to abstract feelings. The movement of fabric, often initiated by wind or by bodies in motion, animates the screen with ephemeral emotion. I investigate how textiles communicate the often hard-to-define sense of anxiety, and particularly the anxiety in trying to figure out what is real and what is not. The figure of the ghost is central in this depiction. I also look at how curtains are important in both expanding and limiting the audience's knowledge, a central concern in the creation of on-screen suspense. Perhaps attributable to the turbulent time in which they were made, the films I examine are especially articulate in their portrayal of the unknown and the unspoken. The large, unfamiliar, and often unmanageable feelings experienced by the characters are translated on screen through the repeated image of blowing textiles.

The unique behaviors of textiles in motion—fluttering; rippling; folding and unfolding—encourage a range of emotional reactions at the same time as they establish the on-screen environment. Fabric, working in conjunction with the film camera, enables cinematographers to control what audiences see and know—the moving fabric of a curtain thwarts our vision, constantly altering what we see. The insubstantial weight, permeability, and unfixed nature of fabric allow for a less defined separation between inside and outside. In addition, the non-rigid material of a window covering means it can move, an important quality for adjusting and changing the audience's view of what is presented on the film screen.

A moving curtain suggests three-dimensional space, indicates the presence of wind, and frames information for the audience. We have long associated our eyes with windows, and filmmakers often use windows to create frames, distancing effects, and reflective surfaces. Windows, like films, present their audiences with limited views of other worlds. Historically, film has drawn on the tension between what is known and what is unknown in order to create suspense and mystery. The unknown, in Western thought and culture, is often associated with groups that have traditionally been "othered." Cinema contributes to this prejudice against the "unknown" by offering restricted, often biased, views into "other" worlds.[6]

Black Narcissus (1947) explores fear and violence alongside eroticized "otherness" in a colonized setting. The film features wind and the presence of wind-blown fabric to paint layers of emotional depth, from desire and despair to malice and menace. The cinematography and mise-en-scène of *Black Narcissus* offers an aesthetically complex presentation achieved in part by the wind and textiles that create suspense in the film.[7] In this and the other films I examine, air and fabric work together to develop on-screen atmosphere.

Kevin L. Ferguson points out that "air's materiality in film is overlooked because it is a materiality with little visuality," adding that "there is no case of air accidentally wandering onto the set; air must be summoned up, cast, given a contract, pampered. For this reason, air is never wasted in a film—the effort alone makes it meaningful."[8] The controlled nature of air on film gives its presence heightened, deliberate meaning. On the film screen we are often shown curtains in movement to effectively communicate the presence of wind. Speaking specifically about Baroque art, Gilles Deleuze reminds us, "the fold is inseparable from wind."[9] While Deleuze is not referencing cinematic representation, the presence of fabric on film does recall the long tradition in art history of suggesting wind with textile folds and drapes in painting and sculpture. Filmmakers, like photographers and painters, employ blowing air to create mood and to give us a sense of the actors' environment. Textiles—for example, as flags, curtains, and dress—help make air and wind visible to audiences to create suspense and mood.

Evoking scent in its title, which refers to "Black Narcissus" perfume, the film announces that intangibility and impermanence, key traits of airborne fragrance, are thematically significant in the film. Sound, too, is associated with air, distance, and sensory impact. Throughout the film, textiles work with sound to show us the persistence of wind and its effect on mood and character. As it was filmed entirely on sets inside film studios, *Black Narcissus* relies on carefully manipulated wind sources. From the start of the film until the end, wind-blown fabric morphs according to the film narrative, adjusting with the plot to indicate danger, changing seasons, or erotic possibility. Gaston Bachelard writes, "each phase of the wind has its own psychology. The wind stirs itself up and becomes discouraged. It howls and groans. It goes from violence to distress. The very nature of the curtailed and useless gusts can give an image of anxious melancholy that is very different from oppressed melancholy."[10] The subtleties Bachelard describes apply to the flexibility of on-screen wind—it can be manipulated and reframed to convey different emotions.

In *Black Narcissus*, a group of English nuns are sent to an abandoned palace high in the Himalayas in the hopes that they will turn it into a school/hospital (and convert the local population). Mr. Dean, the colonial agent stationed at this remote location, writes to the nuns before their arrival, warning them that the "wind blows seven days a week." He observes of this place: "there's something in the atmosphere that makes everything seem exaggerated." A major plot point in *Black Narcissus* is the persistent wind encountered by the relocated nuns—and the "exaggerated," hallucinogenic effect the environment has on them.[11] Instead of repeatedly referencing the wind, or including consistent blowing and whistling sounds, which would be tedious and distracting for the viewer, the filmmakers use background sets that make extensive use of textiles. Even in winter, the windows of the palace remain open, and the gauzy fabric that covers them blows consistently behind and around the actors to show the relentless weather.

When we are first introduced to the Palace of Mopu (also called the "House of Women"), the camera pans to the side of the palace, and curtains shredded by the endless wind blow into the frame. We enter the house through a blowing curtain, and the film cuts to the shadow of a curtain on the wall, where a mural depicts women who once lived there. As we move into the building's interior, we encounter long curtains swaying in a doorway, fabric hanging from ceilings, and leaves blowing along the surfaces of the floors. The curtains are lightweight and worn and frayed from the constant wind. Later, some of the nuns complain that the windows don't shut and the doors won't close. From this introductory scene we learn that wind moves through the entire palace at all times; it is as if the building is a permeable surface—like a loosely woven or fraying textile—rather than a shelter protecting its inhabitants from the weather.

Throughout the film, textiles mark the transitions in mood that accompany turns in the plot. When anticipation turns to suspense, or erotic suggestion turns to nostalgia, we experience, along with the characters, a heightened awareness of sensation, usually accompanied by an increase in wind. A sudden rustling of the curtains might signal a tremor of emotion in the actors. For example, the departure of Sister Philippa coincides with a growing sense of chaos and a fear of Sister Clodagh's loosening grip on the mountaintop community. The sound of howling wind and the image of blowing nun habits mark this moment of growing tension.

As the leader and protagonist of the film, Sister Clodagh is engaged in a fruitless struggle to control her environment. Revealing the rising hysteria of the nuns, an early scene shows us Sister Briony, robes billowing, visiting Sister Clodagh's curtain-filled room to warn of Sister Ruth's increasing loss of mental stability. Sister Clodagh blames Ruth's illness on "this wind": the unceasing blowing air that surrounds them. One of the film's concerns is with a weakening of the boundary between physical and mental life. The permeability of the palace walls signifies the nuns' vulnerability to the emotions they previously attempted to keep at bay, namely: desire, jealousy, and violence.

The concept of exposure in *Black Narcissus* takes on multiple meanings. Throughout the film, we are reminded of the persistent wind on the mountain and how it disrupts and disturbs the nuns who have relocated there. Perched on the side of a mountain, the house is vulnerable to the wind in all seasons. On a less literal level, the character of Mr. Dean sparks a different kind of exposure. Often appearing in a state of partial undress, Mr. Dean is the catalyst for Sister Clodagh's confession of past heartbreak, and for Sister Ruth's erotically charged breakdown at the end of the film. In contrast to the nuns' full habits and robes, Mr Dean's costuming is carefree, comfortable, and suited to the elements. His chest and legs are often unclothed, and he accepts the lack of social and environmental order that surrounds them. The combination of physical freedom and relaxed attitude makes Mr. Dean both tempting and threatening to the asexual, strict lives of the nuns. He and Sister Clodagh confide in each other, sharing a near-intimacy that eventually breaks the

Figure 5.2 Two nuns commiserating in the palace. Credit: *Black Narcissus* (dir. Michael Powell and Emeric Pressburger, 1947), ITV Global Entertainment Ltd.

heightened tension that has built throughout the film. Like the palace exposed to the winds, Mr. Dean's emotional openness forces the nuns into a vulnerability that they cannot bear.

Black Narcissus relies on the motif of blowing wind to depict the intersections of desire, fear, sexuality, and madness. Inaccessible bodies, dead bodies, and projected bodies haunt the screen, combining suppressed eroticism with suspense and uncertainty. An image of blowing curtains can suggest a presence where there is none; on film, apparitions are often figured as filmy, pale-colored fabric forms moved by air. Among the multiple cinematic effects created by the image of blowing curtains, a sense of ghostliness or otherworldliness can be used to develop a mysterious or suspenseful plot point.

Even in films that may not be explicitly about ghosts, textiles can create a sense of haunting or the spectral in a way that gives life to

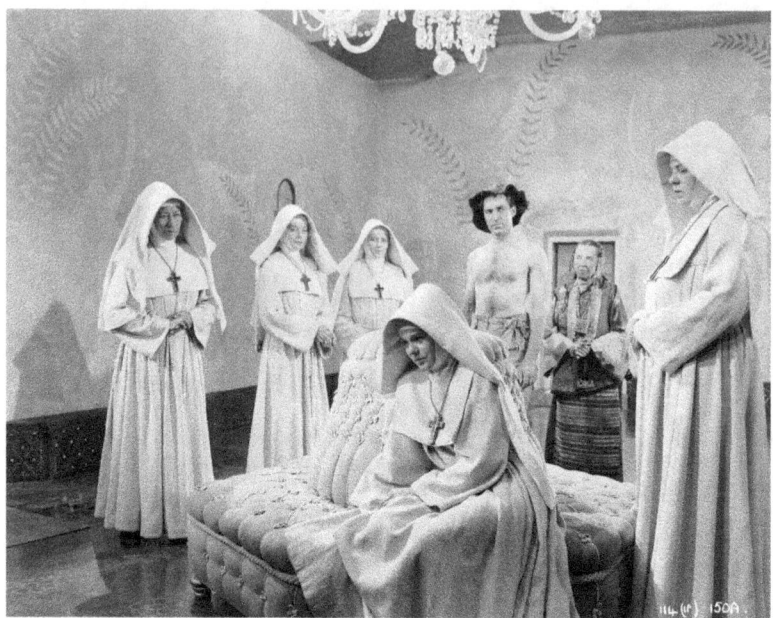

Figure 5.3 David Farrar, as Mr. Dean, his exposed skin contrasting with the nuns' heavy garments, in *Black Narcissus*, 1947. Courtesy Getty Images UK.

the lifeless. In this way, on-screen textiles materialize the intangible, including abstract emotions and ideas—memory, death, coincidence, and magic, to name a few examples. The ethereal motion of moving fabric serves as a sort of placeholder for concepts that are unexplained, irrational, taboo, and/or not understood. On film, giving visibility to the unknown and to complex emotions is crucial in communicating mood and character development, as well as in creating a multi-layered story and screen.

Ghostliness—the unstable place between life and death—is central to *Rebecca* (1940, dir. Alfred Hitchcock). The film's narrator is haunted by her husband's first wife, the now-dead (and faceless) Rebecca. Throughout the film, both wives are simultaneously present and absent.[12] While the dead Rebecca haunts the narrative, the current wife is also ghostly. We know the narrator by her voice and her appearance, but never learn her name. Like Rebecca, it is as if she is both present and absent in the house. This haunting effect—specifically, the narrator's absence and the uncanny presence of Rebecca—is made possible in part by the use of curtaining, especially in her scene with the housekeeper Mrs. Danvers in Rebecca's bedroom, untouched since her death.

The initial voiceover of the film features the narrator describing a dream in which she returns to the Manderley estate. Outside the house, she is blocked by the iron gate that opens onto the estate grounds. She explains: "I was possessed of sudden, supernatural powers and passed like a spirit through the barrier before me." This illustrates the narrator's ghostly quality—she is without physical body, and, speaking from the future, is able to transcend the lines between dream and reality, and to breach the physical barrier of the gate. The filmic medium, in which sound/voice is separated from image, enables this phantom-like presence. Her movement through the gate and into Manderley prefigures the later scene, in which wind blows curtains across the window sills and into the interior of Rebecca's room.

In *Rebecca* the characters are constantly approaching, veering away from, and/or transcending physical, social, and other boundaries. The narrator's lower-class background and ignorance of the history of Manderley puts her at constant risk of offending others and humiliating herself. Her innocence about how to act and what to say, and her sense that she is, in the eyes of those around her, a childish and unserious wife for Maxim de Winter, increases her anxiety. Much of the nervousness evoked by the film revolves around the possibility that her words or actions might result in social transgression. Her relationship with Mrs. Danvers is particularly fraught with tension.

We see this when she ventures into Rebecca's former room and is surprised by Mrs. Danvers: the props of the room highlight its strange in-between state, while alerting us to Mrs. Danvers's continued longing for Rebecca. The room is sepulchral, maintained by Mrs. Danvers to remain just how it was when Rebecca died, making it a taboo space for the new wife. In one cut, we move abruptly from the wind-filled curtains to the appearance of Mrs. Danvers standing behind sheer room dividers, as if she herself had just blown into the room. It is as if Mrs. Danvers, too, is possessed by Rebecca's ghost. The tall window curtains, which create dynamic patterns of light and shadow, and the fabric of Rebecca's underwear and pillowcase (lovingly admired by Mrs. Danvers), are infused with Rebecca's absent body. More broadly, the narrator is horrified by her own lack of presence in the room and in the house—she sees that she is unable to animate or spark desire as Rebecca once did. This anxiety culminates at the end of the film when, prompted by Mrs. Danvers, she unknowingly dresses herself in a way that seems to conjure Rebecca's ghost.[13]

Absent, ghostly bodies brought to life by wind-blown curtains haunt film history. The presence of curtains on film is also a reference

Figure 5.4 Judith Anderson as Mrs. Danvers. Credit: *Rebecca* (dir. Alfred Hitchcock, 1940), ABC, Inc.

to curtains as they appear on the theatrical stage and in the history of performance. On-stage curtains restrict the viewer's point of view, increasing suspense and a sense of mystery regarding what is happening off-stage. In addition to this visual framing, theatrical curtaining works to separate the real life of the audience space from the fantastical world presented on stage. Curtains therefore offer filmmakers opportunities to present and explore tensions between fantasy and reality, surrealism and naturalism, performer and spectator, art and life.

As an everyday architectural element, curtains are important markers of the divide between private and public spaces.[14] They can be moved back and forth across a window and can be crafted from materials that either prohibit or allow air and light. These qualities enable curtains to control outsiders' knowledge of a closed-off world. The use of ripped, loose-weave fabrics such as the curtains in *Black Narcissus* reflect the "frayed" nerves and gradual decline experienced by the emotionally fragile nuns. The decision to leave the curtains in their porous, neglected state—despite the fact that the nuns are increasingly tormented by the wind and would seem to benefit from sturdy curtains—conveys the nuns' increasing instability. On the frayed or fraying textile, Catherine Dormor writes: "sometimes they are mended or darned, but sometimes left frayed as a conscious tactic of aesthetics or memory."[15] Dormor and Julia Bryan-Wilson's contributions to the topic of frayage are important interventions into this particularly fiber-based "state," and offer new viewpoints on how we might "read" frayed cloth through political and philosophical contexts. The curtains "left frayed" in *Black Narcissus* are perhaps more literal—their foregrounding in the film points to the defeated, fatigued mentality of the palace inhabitants, who are worn down by the persistent winds.

Window coverings regulate privacy: visual access to building interiors can be adjusted to shut out those who are unwelcome or unfamiliar to those inside. On stage, too, they can limit the viewer's knowledge: they hide and expose, controlling which information is available to the audience, and mark transitions in and out of fantastical worlds.[16] Stage curtains signal movement into and out of live performance, letting audience members know when they should assume the listener/observer "role" in the theatrical space. They enclose the performers and the (often fictional) worlds they inhabit. The characteristics of domestic and theatrical curtaining extend into the cinematic mise-en-scène.

While the depiction of curtains on film incorporates these two histories—the history of curtains as everyday domestic object and that of theatrical curtaining—it is also complicated by the technology of the film camera. Unlike our daily experience of seeing through and using windows and curtains, viewing curtains on film demands that we consider how camera and textile work together to communicate meaning, via editing cuts, framing, and composition.

While wind-blown curtains in *Black Narcissus* heighten on-screen suspense and those in *Rebecca* emphasize a ghostly tension between presence and absence, hanging fabric in *La Belle et la Bête* (dir. Jean Cocteau, 1946) plays a different role—one that evokes a sense of wonder and fantasy. Based on a French story from the mid-1700s, the film follows the economic and romantic ascent of Belle, whose beloved father steals a rose from the Beast's castle and agrees to send Belle to the Beast as repayment. At first repulsed by the Beast, Belle gradually falls in love with him. The film suggests this growing affection in part through magical, whimsical details and camera tricks.

The story of *La Belle et la Bête* references its eighteenth-century Baroque origins in its depictions of moving fabric. Baroque art celebrated the seemingly endless, unrealistic movement of folded fabric. Pennina Barnett describes Baroque sculptor Gian Lorenzo Bernini's work "The Ecstasy of Saint Teresa": in the sculpture, "folds that cannot be explained by the body, multiply and become autonomous. We are in the Baroque. A period of swathing draperies and billowing clothes."[17] Reading cultural perceptions of "swathing draperies and billowing clothes" across different time periods and technologies—from Baroque sculpture to twentieth-century film—reveals the lasting impact of this specific aesthetic detail. A sense of marvel at "capturing" fabric movement expressed in marble is retained in the seemingly miraculous movement of objects, including textiles, on film. The physically impossible abundance of the folds of "Saint Teresa" is a useful entry point into Cocteau's Baroque-era fairy tale, which, in its cinematic translation, echoes the sculpture's nonsensical, "impossible" quality and creates awe in its viewer.

Cocteau's film interpretation of *La Belle et la Bête* is celebrated for its innovative use of moving props in creating an otherworldly mise-en-scène. Objects such as anthropomorphized candleholders in the interior of the Beast's home move and respond without animated special effects, suggesting the presence of magic. Curtaining signals Belle's movement in and out of the Beast's world, charting her transition into marriage and its accompanying economic security. In many versions of this story, including Jean Cocteau's cinematic one, there is a marked contrast between the financial struggles of Belle's life with her family and the lavish lifestyle offered by the Beast. Curtains help carry us along on Belle's journey into an unfamiliar life with the Beast.

In her dreary reality, she cleans while wearing ragged clothing, Cinderella-like, while her sisters assert their class superiority by wearing voluminous dresses with excessive amounts of rich fabric and ornamentation. At the start of the film, their cruelty toward Belle is partially expressed in their solid class separation and their devotion to lives of leisure. The family's sudden loss of fortune and Belle's gradual attachment to the wealthy Beast result in a reversal of roles. Near the end of *La Belle et la Bête*, after Belle has established her dedication to the Beast and wears his gifts of luxurious dresses, veils, and jewels, she returns home to find her sisters mired in domestic labor. Rows of seemingly endless white sheets hanging on clothes lines hide the sisters, who are now forced to do their own laundry. Trapped in a labyrinth of daily chores, the sisters react with rage and envy at Belle's display of riches.

We are ushered into the transitional space between Belle's reality with her family and her new life with the Beast by curtain-like props. Belle's father, running to and from the Beast's house in the forest, is guided in and out by moving tree branches that bend to the side like curtains to conceal him as he leaves. This portrays the Beast's lair as a theatrical, fantastical environment. Similarly, Belle's first experience of the Beast's home resembles a stage entrance, as she steps into a stage-like place of uncertain space and time. When Belle first enters the Beast's castle in the forest, she runs through doorways and halls, and her body moves next to the wind-blown fabrics in the building's

Figure 5.5 Josette Day as Belle, wearing gifts from the Beast in *La Belle et la Bête*, 1946. Courtesy Getty Images UK.

interior. At this moment in *La Belle et la Bête*, Belle leaves the world of her father and ventures into the unfamiliar—she is poised on a sort of threshold.

Thomas Elsaesser and Malte Hagener explain how the concept of the "threshold" is used to describe the viewer's relationship to the film screen. A "threshold" in film "always has two sides, as it simultaneously connects and separates—a border can be crossed precisely because a division always implies spatial proximity."[18] Presented with a threshold on screen, the viewer knows there is the potential for the camera to take them across the border, into the unknown space on the other side of the frame. *La Belle et la Bête* utilizes curtaining, windows, doors, as well as glass and mirrors, to delineate the threshold between reality and the magical world of the Beast. It is by passing through these "frames" that we access worlds beyond our real lives. The motion of curtains across a stage or window determines the borders between private and public, interior and exterior, fantasy and reality. Filmmakers seeking to portray secrecy, danger, surprise, and other emotions rely on these longstanding performance traditions.

As Açalya Allmer writes, the curtain "remains as a symbol of theater and retains its power as a metaphor for the transformation between everyday and stage life."[19] Belle's first experience of the Beast's castle is marked by atmospheric use of wind and fabric, and suggests a moment of "transformation between everyday and stage life." Blowing fabrics inside the home give us a sense of Belle's point-of-view as she explores the house for the first time. During this scene Belle transitions to the "stage" or "magic" world of her new life with the Beast. Moving through the Beast's entryway, Belle runs in a long cape. Slow-motion cinematography shows us her cape's dramatic folds and reminds us that the laws of time and space do not apply here. We are constantly reminded that this is a crafted environment in which the camera and cinematic technology are essential to creating illusion. The cape billows dramatically around Belle throughout the scene as she runs through the house. The blowing drapery of the cape is echoed in the hallway scene, where wind blows a row of sheer white window curtains. Occasionally illuminating Belle's face from an outside light source, the curtains are both welcoming and menacing, surrounding Belle as she moves closer and closer to the camera.

Figure 5.6 Josette Day as Belle in *La Belle et la Bête*, 1946. Courtesy Getty Images UK.

In experimental films that are made and distributed outside conventional Hollywood, wind-blown textiles also work to establish mood and convey meaning—but are not necessarily concerned with traditional plot and character development. Seeing curtaining as significant prop in terms of its materiality or its textural parallel with the film screen offers viewers insights into art not tied to storytelling. Imagining the film strip itself as a surface which can be designed and imprinted has led to experiments with color, layering, and depth.[20]

Avant-garde films, and particularly films exploring queer culture and identity, have long examined themes of theatricality and excess in form and content.[21] One influential example that makes significant use of curtaining is Kenneth Anger's 1949 short film *Puce Moment*, which employs curtaining to investigate cinematic history and form.[22] *Puce Moment* includes intricate décor and inconsistent camera speeds to develop, as Matthew Tinkcom writes, "a textural cinema driven mostly through the camp affection for the look and shimmer of fabric, jewelry, and ornamentation."[23] At times a jerky, shaking camera (mimicking silent film techniques) mirrors the movement of the sparkling fabrics displayed in the film.

In the opening scene of *Puce Moment*, a static camera records the torsos of a group of 1920s dresses (in reality a gift from Anger's grandmother, a former Hollywood costumer). Held from above and wiggled as they approach the camera, the colorful dresses, some sequined and beaded, take turns and move in formation, not unlike dancers in a Broadway show or a musical film production. Because the dresses are removed from bodies (even the hand that holds them up is outside the frame), they have a curtain-like—and ghost-like—quality.

Gen Doy points out: "such is the close relationship between the body and clothing that a sense of lack is apparent when we view clothes which are not being worn or displayed on models."[24] Rather than developing an explicit narrative about the places the dresses had been and the people who wore them, Anger uses this "lack" to pay homage to the materiality of silent cinema: the cinematography and mise-en-scène assume the unique characteristics and forms of 1920s Hollywood filmmaking. A focus on the dresses themselves, rather than those who once wore them, encourages us to study them as crafted objects reflecting the available technology at the time of their making. The dresses in *Puce Moment* contain the potential for "being worn or displayed," and, like the other examples of blowing curtains and textiles I have examined in this chapter, the presence of moving dresses without bodies has a haunting presence. As with other used or vintage items, we might imagine who wore the dress before it was abandoned.

In *Puce Moment* we assume the viewpoint of the to-be-revealed actress who is looking through her dresses and deciding which one to wear. The static camera records the process of selection: we sift through the garments as we determine which item to choose. This process involves paying detailed attention to the colors, textures, and ornamentation of each garment that passes in front of our eyes. Like many of Anger's films, *Puce Moment* does not have dialogue—the soundtrack is our primary experience of sound. As a result we are not drawn into characters' voices and conversations; instead, we are brought into a state of reverie, immersed in the highly personal intimacies of color and light—the moving fabric creates an experience of three-dimensional space.[25]

Recalling the filmed serpentine dances from the early twentieth century, *Puce Moment* evokes the theatrical roots of fabric and curtaining in motion. Films such as *La Belle et la Bête*, *Rebecca*, and *Black Narcissus* bring elements of theatrical curtaining into their costuming and décor, and at the same time incorporate textiles to move the plot forward and develop suspense and delight. Often when the focus is not on straightforward storytelling, as in *Puce Moment*, a film can bring added significance to cinematic material and the actual process of making a film. In my conclusion I return to this question of materiality and film, and how we might think about issues around labor and textiles in digital media.

Conclusion

Digital Experimentation and the Legacy of the Handmade

Films such as *Puce Moment*, often categorized as avant-garde or experimental, are foundational to my explorations of material presence on film and the framing and filming of textiles. My initial investigations into textiles on film began, over a decade ago, with a study of Maya Deren's groundbreaking film *Meshes of the Afternoon* (1943).[1] Deren's ideas about process, tactility, and interiority, as well as her use of fabric, have continued to inform my thinking. Textiles have long played an important role in developing cinematic effects—especially regarding intimacy, mood, and sensory experience, as I have shown—that challenge the restrictions of mainstream film. As I am indebted to the thinking prompted by avant-garde artists, especially around labor and innovation, I want to conclude with two brief examples of fabric on experimental film which continue to stretch and complicate my interdisciplinary approach. Deren's *Ritual in Transfigured Time* (1945–6) and Jodie Mack's *Posthaste Perennial Pattern* (2010) resonate with many of the questions I have asked while "reading" textiles on film. At the same time, both films pose relevant questions about future cinematic and fiber-based innovation.

Deren's experimental silent film *Ritual in Transfigured Time* focuses on how film editing refigures dance and choreography while examining the tension between the individual and the collective. Throughout the film, we watch the camera slow, speed, and cut as it records multiple gatherings and social interactions. We witness intimacy and connection as well as obstacles to communication. While we cannot hear the voices of the actors/dancers, their bodies convey emotion and drama. Deren, who is not just the director but also a central performer in her own film, presents ideas about women, performance, and power which I return to again and again.

Deren's fifteen-minute film contains within it many of the questions I have been asking throughout these chapters. Employing nonverbal means to convey emotional depth and the nuances of intimacy, separation, and distance, through props and the use of cinematic space, is a central concern of my examination of the interrelation of textiles and film. The forces of attraction and repulsion, and their accompanying physical and tactile experiences, are on visual display in *Ritual in Transfigured Time*. Motion, as represented in dancing bodies, rotating yarn, blowing fabric, and slow motion and freeze editing effects, builds a multidimensional screen, a significant point I discuss in Chapter 5. Deren also considers the various meanings of suspense as they can be developed on screen: the prohibition of knowledge, suspended/stopped time, as well as the literal suspension of bodies, at the end of the film. These entangled themes start with an image of textile making.

To introduce the film, Deren depicts herself winding yarn, first by herself, then accompanied by another dancer (Rita Christiani). We move back and forth between the two women with the yarn or twine between them. The camera slows to show Deren's back-and-forth movement (she holds the yarn in outstretched hands) in detail, documenting the mechanics of preparing yarn for knitting. Her growing emotion and ecstatic rocking suggest an increasing joy and sense of spiritual enlightenment. Deren's foregrounding of the ritual of winding thread further emphasizes how the technologies of film and textile-making alter our experience of time. This presentation of tactile-informed work, part of the repetitive labor involved in textile-making, has been central in my thinking about the depiction of labor and tactility on the film screen.

Another short film that exemplifies the avant-garde's foregrounding of materiality through textiles is experimental filmmaker and animator Jodie Mack's 16-mm film *Posthaste Perennial Pattern*. This short (less than four minutes) film consists of a series of close-ups of different synthetic fabrics printed with floral patterns. Building on the themes presented in *Ritual in Transfigured Time*, *Posthaste Perennial Pattern* merges textiles and film in a way that requires audiences to consider craft in relation to technology, and to acknowledge the work that goes into fabric-making and filmmaking.

The floral prints in *Posthaste Perennial Pattern* are dynamic: quick cuts animate the printed flowers, blending one into the next as they swirl around the screen. Textile designs, as shown in Mack's film, can be loosened from their original or intended usage and take on new resonances as they inhabit different environments. These messages extend beyond the body to printed fabric on interior and exterior walls, curtaining, and upholstery. The proximity of the fabrics to the camera enables us to see their texture and weave, reminding us that we are watching a film, not viewing the textiles in everyday use. We see them as a filmmaker (or a dressmaker) might—in close examination and removed from context, rather than as part of a garment or an element of interior décor. This intimate quality forces us to consider the textile itself and how it was framed by the filmmaker, recalling the detailed processes of sewing and quilting: cutting, measuring, and imagining patterns in relation to each other. Considering the role of the film camera and film technology in framing and manipulating how we see and experience textiles has been important, as I look at not just the recording of textiles but the specific impact of looking at fabrics through a cinematic lens.

Posthaste Perennial Pattern does not utilize textiles to develop plot and/or character as part of an overall mood or story, as many of the films I examine in previous chapters do. But Mack's short film does call attention to questions, primarily in my chapter on polyester, about the tensions between "natural" and artifice, handmade and machine-made. *Posthaste Perennial Pattern*'s presence in the Museum of Arts and Design's exhibit on Miriam Shapiro (the 2018 "Surface/ Depth: The Decorative After Miriam Shapiro," curated by Elissa Auther) positions the film alongside other artists who investigate the political impact of craft, class, and labor, and particularly women's relationships with textiles.[2]

I bring up these films here because I feel they encapsulate many of the issues I have confronted while studying the relationship between textiles and film. Looking closely at fiber-based material, as Mack does in her film, forces us to pay attention to details such as the construction of the weave. The multifaceted senses and emotions associated with textiles—including touch, longing/desire, repulsion, non-verbal communication, movement, and texture—demand an approach that refuses to erase the "making" aspect of filmmaking.[3] I consistently find this careful attention to making in the work of directors who operate outside the Hollywood system.[4]

Returning to questions about labor I posed in the introduction chapter, I want to ask again how we might think about film as a made, crafted object—and particularly how we might imagine film "work" and "making" during an age of increasingly digital filmmaking. *Posthaste Perennial Pattern*, a handmade experimental film using an older technology (16-mm film), intervenes in a productive way in this discussion of making. Mack's film draws a link between makers of film and makers of fabrics, asking questions about work, use, value, and the history of technology.[5] Deren's film, too, acknowledges the filmmaker as worker and performer, referencing back to Vertov's image of the film editor in *Man with a Movie Camera* (the 1929 avant-garde film which began my Introduction chapter).

Much of mainstream film, fully embracing digital technology, seeks to make the work behind filmmaking as invisible as possible. The advent of digital film has brought increased attention to issues concerning the surface of the screen, such as depth, texture, and the effects of pixelation. Recent developments in "smart" textiles often incorporate cinematic qualities such as light and movement into the material. Considering the role of fabric in innovative media points toward an increasingly interdependent and productive relationship between fiber-based material and the world of the projected image. Debates about the role of computers and coding in the fields of weaving, craft, and textile design are relevant to these recent advances in screen technology.[6] There has been a wave of new scholarship about the interrelations of pixelation, craft, textiles, and digital media.[7] While I have not discussed animation in this book, the possibilities in creating new forms of tactility and textures in digital animated media presents additional questions about the film/textile connection.

My readings emerge from a tradition of film analysis in which scholars and filmmakers imagine the audience in a traditional public film theater setting, featuring a film projected on a screen in front of the seated viewers. Contemporary experience is quite different and much more tactile—we hold and touch our screens constantly, and we look at much smaller screens. How might this more physically intimate experience of film-watching impact how we examine and write about film and about fabrics on film? How will the cinematic portrayal of evocative, textured textiles and other materials adjust to this context?

Exploring materiality in digital forms raises important questions for film and textile scholars. I wonder, for example, how changing photographic technologies will impact future exhibits, books, and other publications in the field of textile studies. What role will textile makers and designers play in digital film production? In addition, as digital film aims for more and more realistic-looking touchable surfaces, how might this alter how we see handmade textiles and other craft objects? How will the medium of film portray the human work behind fabric-making and filmmaking? And how can we continue to acknowledge the human labor, as well as the history of film technologies, that is central in the creation of new forms of media?

While the move away from the physicality of the film strip has led many to lament the craft of filmmaking, in fact digital film forces directors to examine and utilize the handmade in innovative ways, including creative use of the woven as prop and metaphor. I look forward to reading future projects more specific than my own, as well as accounts by practitioners of both textiles and film, that will provide valuable thinking about the potential for materiality in digital forms.[8]

Textiles are deeply embedded in cultural objects and traditions. The processes of fabric-making have woven their way into our language, and they will inevitably impact filmmaking's rapidly moving technological change. Writing in 1997, Sadie Plant points to the persistence of fabric in new media forms:

> If textiles appear to lose touch with their weaving spells and spans of time, they also continue to fabricate the very screens with which they are concealed. And because these are processes, they keep processing . . . weaving wends its way through even the media which supplant it.[9]

Plant recognizes the trace of textile-making "through even the media which supplant it." The qualities of fabrics emerge as through a palimpsest, asserting their presence even after society deems them obsolete. I also look to Giuliana Bruno's theory of "technological alchemy":

> With regard to materiality, I aim to demonstrate that the physicality of a thing one can touch does not vanish with the disappearance of its material but can morph culturally, transmuting into another medium. I like to call this technological alchemy, and

see it occurring on the surface of different media. Such alchemic transformation is occurring, for example, with the passing of celluloid. A form of materiality returns to the screen at the moment of film's obsolescence, traveling on the surface of other media. In the digital age, materiality can be reactivated, because it was always a virtual condition.[10]

Bruno, like Plant, argues that emerging technological forms potentially contain their own material histories. A "reactivation" of materiality reframes our understanding of the messages and influence of fabric—and reading through textiles will, I hope, inspire further discussion of the material and historical conditions of filmmaking. A layered, textured media infused with history makes for rich analysis, and times of technological transition produce potential and promise alongside obsolescence. As we move into unknown realms of making and experimentation, the intertwining relationship between textiles and films will continue to shape and transform how we see the world.

Notes

Preface

1 Sabrina Gschwandtner, "Knitting Is . . .," in *The Textiles Reader*, ed. Jessica Hemmings (London: Bloomsbury, 2012), 409.

Introduction

1 In the Introduction to *Kino-Eye: The Writings of Dziga Vertov*, Annette Michelson gives additional context for Vertov's linking of industry, commerce, and machinery through film editing technique: "Now it is Vertov's positioning of film-as-production within the cyclical and parallel structure of his cinematic discourse and his insistence on the simultaneous and related revolutions of the wheels of industry and transportation and of the cranks and spindles of the filmmaking apparatus that establishes, through the first two-thirds of his film-text, the general relation of film production to other sectors of labor. The editing structure has through the first two-thirds of the film established a rhythmic pulsing of energy that binds together the movements of industrial labor (the work of mason, ax-grinder, garment manufacturer, miner, switchboard operator, cigarette maker). The editing structure culminates in the identification of filmmaking (presented throughout the film in the full range of its productive processes: editing, laboratory processing, and exhibition, as well as camera work) as now directly and explicitly related to the paradigmatic form of industry: textile manufacture, itself seen as central in the economy's production." Annette Michelson, Introduction, *Kino-Eye: The Writings of Dziga Vertov* (Berkeley: University of California Press, 1985), xxxviii-xxxviiii.

2   Rebecca Solnit, *River of Shadows: Eadweard Muybridge and the Technological Wild West* (New York: Penguin, 2003), 22.

3   As Esther Leslie writes, "there are many ways in which the language and practice of film are analogous to the modes of fabric, ranging from the montage and cutting techniques that build up a film, just as cutting and stitching make clothing, to the technological fact that both were boosted by the expansion of the plastics industry." Esther Leslie, "Dreams for Sale," in *Birds of Paradise: Costume as Cinematic Spectacle*, ed. Marketa Uhlirova (London: Koenig Books, 2013), 34.

4   Personal email correspondence with Mary Lance, April 19, 2018.

5   Walter Murch, *In the Blink of an Eye: A Perspective on Film Editing*, 2nd ed. (Los Angeles: Silman-James Press, 2001), 49.

6   Erin Hill, *Never Done: A History of Women's Work in Media Production* (New Brunswick: Rutgers University Press, 2016), 5.

7   Ibid., 73.

8   David Meuel points out that this work assignment changed in the 1920s: "Female film editors and assistants, who could easily land jobs in cutting rooms during the 1910s, were told that this work was now too taxing for them physically, passed over for advancement, and urged to give up their jobs so men could have them." In *Women Film Editors: Unseen Artists of American Cinema* (Jefferson: McFarland & Company, 2016), 1.

9   Mise-en-scène can be thought of as a kind of curated space. Close examination of the fiber-based surfaces and arrangement of film props often reveals a carefully constructed composition. Within the curated scene of the film frame, directors, set designers, art directors, and production designers build meaning with objects, color, and spatial relationships. Judith Clark, in an essay on curating and museums, tells us: "curating is a way of thinking about spatial analogies." "Statement VI," in *The Textiles Reader*, ed. Jessica Hemmings (London: Bloomsbury, 2012), 194. I am interested in how we might think of the film set as a network of spatial analogies, curated by filmmakers and designers.

10 The dynamic nature of tapestry is proto-cinematic in its ability to convey stories using elements of time and space. Anne Hollander discusses the proto-cinematic, particularly in reference to painting, in

Moving Pictures; she writes about "a search through the history of art for the kinds of picture that attempted and prefigured what cinema later actually did, and that form a background and foundation for movies." (Cambridge, MA: Harvard University Press, 1991), 4.

11 Glenn Adamson, *The Invention of Craft* (London: Bloomsbury, 2013), xiii.

12 Anni Albers, "Constructing Textiles" (1946, revised 1959), in *Anni Albers; Selected Writings on Design*, ed. Brenda Danilowitz (Hanover: Wesleyan University Press, 2001), 33.

13 Kathleen Morris, "You Are Not a Lemming: The Imagined Resistance of Craft Citizenship," *The Journal of Modern Craft* 9, no. 1 (2016): 6–7.

14 T'ai Smith, "The Problem with Craft," *Art Journal* 75, no. 1 (2016): 80. The book *The New Politics of the Handmade: Craft, Art and Design* (London: Bloomsbury, 2020) also takes up this issue.

15 Glenn Adamson, *Thinking Through Craft* (London: Bloomsbury, 2007), 5.

16 Naomi Schor, *Reading in Detail: Aesthetics and the Feminine* (New York: Routledge, 2007), 15.

17 Vivian Sobchack, *Carnal Thoughts: Embodiment and Moving Image Culture* (Berkeley: University of California Press, 2004), 59.

18 Laura U. Marks, *The Skin of the Film: Intercultural Cinema, Embodiment, and the Senses* (Durham: Duke University Press, 2000), 162. Marks explains how her definition of "haptic" originates with the art historian Aloïs Riegl, a textile curator: "One can imagine how the hours spent inches away from the weave of a carpet might have stimulated the art historian's ideas about a close-up and tactile way of looking." From *Touch: Sensuous Theory and Multisensory Media* (Minneapolis: University of Minnesota Press, 2002), 4.

19 My approach also follows Thomas Elsaesser and Malte Hagener, who assert: "our trajectory through film theory deliberately avoids setting up a categorical distinction between the cinema experience as a theatrical event and the cinema experience as an ambient event, no more than it posits a radical break between analogue and digital film. Instead, it maps the respective (and salient) differences of various film theories around changing—new and not-so-new—configurations of

the spectator's body and senses." Thomas Elsaesser and Malte Hagener, *Film Theory: An Introduction Through the Senses*, 2nd ed. (New York: Routledge, 2015), 5.

20 Eugenie Brinkema, *The Forms of the Affects* (Durham: Duke University Press, 2014), xv. Scholarly interest in materiality has turned to philosophers Gilles Deleuze and Félix Guattari, particularly in reference to rethinking texture, surface, and the fold—this method of analysis has also informed my viewpoint. The fold as a mode of theoretical interpretation, through Deleuze, has emerged as an important way to interrogate film and materiality. See Gilles Deleuze, *The Fold: Leibniz and the Baroque*, trans. Tom Conley (Minneapolis: University of Minnesota Press, 1993) and Gilles Deleuze and Félix Guattari, "1440: The Smooth and the Striated," in *A Thousand Plateaus: Capitalism and Schizophrenia*, trans. Brian Massumi (Minneapolis: University of Minnesota Press, 1987). In order to bring theories of the fold into this study, it has been useful for me to literalize "the fold" somewhat, as I am concerned primarily with issues of light on drapery and the visual effects of folded fabric. The three-dimensional, sculptural quality of draped fabric is central to creating a sense of depth on the flat screen. Scholars such as Gen Doy have provided important studies on the use of drapery in art; the particular technology of the moving image, however, presents new questions about the function of folded fabric. See also Giuliana Bruno, *Surface: Matters of Aesthetics, Materiality, and Media* (Chicago: University of Chicago Press, 2014) and Saige Walton, *Cinema's Baroque Flesh: Film, Phenomenology and the Art of Entanglement* (Amsterdam: Amsterdam University Press, 2016).

21 Schor, *Reading in Detail*, xlvii.

22 Ibid., xlv.

23 Psychoanalysis, while not central to my readings, does inform my examination of culture and desire, and is particularly relevant in the chapters where I deal with fetish, desire, and memory. Much of Valerie Steele's work is informed by psychoanalysis; see, for example, *Fetish: Fashion, Sex & Power* (Oxford University Press, 1997) and *The Corset: A Cultural History* (New Haven: Yale University Press, 2001). See also

Alison Bancroft, Fashion and Psychoanalysis (London: I.B. Tauris, 2012) and *Thinking Through Fashion: A Guide to Key Theorists*, ed. Agnès Rocamora and Anneke Smelik (London: I.B. Tauris, 2015).

24 Salomé Aguilera Skvirsky's book *The Process Genre: Cinema and the Aesthetic of Labor* (Durham: Duke University Press 2020) deals specifically with these types of films. The British Film Institute's online collection *Textiles on Film* includes many examples of labor films (and specifically textile labor in the U.K): https://player.bfi.org.uk/free/collection/textiles-on-film. Accessed 2.4.21.

25 Roland Barthes, *The Language of Fashion*, trans. Andy Stafford (London: Bloomsbury, 2013), 26.

26 I acknowledge some issues are beyond the scope of this project. My approach is not grounded in archival research, as I do not have institutional funding to support work in archives, so the exact textiles I reference are based on my knowledge as a film viewer rather than on actual, close contact with archival film costuming and décor. Because I am naming fabrics according to what appears on the screen, not touching costuming or examining textiles in person, there may be some inaccuracies regarding the quality and authenticity of the fabrics I discuss. My analysis lacks references to many cinematic and fiber-based artworks around the globe. My hope is that this mode of reading textiles and film will help inform in-depth, specific studies that draw from wider fields of expertise than my own.

27 Hillel Schwartz speaks about fantasy in the content of films, noting that early films "made a point of being synthetic" and "most features reveled in artifice: miraculous escapes, leaps of the calendar, outbreaks of singing and dancing." *The Culture of the Copy: Striking Likenesses, Unreasonable Facsimiles* (New York: Zone Books, 1996), 196.

Chapter 1

1 Elena Phipps, *Looking at Textiles: A Guide to Technical Terms* (Los Angeles: J. Paul Getty Museum, 2011), 67.

2   Ibid.
3   Anni Albers, "The Fundamental Constructions," in *On Weaving* (Princeton: Princeton University Press, 2017), 27. In this essay Albers also writes of satin and plain weaves: "The contrast to the plain weave becomes apparent again when we compare the possible functions of the two; for, whereas we considered the plain weave to be the most serviceable construction, the satin weave is a luxurious one. The soft drape, the gloss that usually goes with the weave, and on the negative side, the long floating threads that preclude hard wear predispose it for an extravagant existence. It is a weave made for splendor. We know it in the form of silk satin, used in decorous draperies or, equally decorously, in our clothes of leisure." (28)
4   Phipps, *Looking at Textiles*, 51.
5   For more on modernism and the use of light as a type of "material," see Laszlo Moholy-Nagy, *Painting, Photography, Film*, trans. Janet Seligman (London: Lund Humphries, 1967).
6   Gen Doy argues for the importance of drapery in the modern age, paying special attention to Madame Grès: "in Vionnet's work, the dress and body are in close contact and Vionnet rejected the idea of corsets and other foundation garments" (86), and "[Grès] attempted to make the body and cloth a seamless entity" (91). Gen Doy, *Drapery: Classicism and Barbarism in Visual Culture* (London: I.B. Tauris, 2002).
7   Harold Koda says that "by positioning the fabric diagonally, the warp and weft of the cloth is turned into true bias, an angle of increased elasticity." *Goddess: The Classical Mode* (New Haven: Yale University Press and New York: The Metropolitan Museum of Art, 2003), 68.
8   "Not only had exercise and sport become increasingly popular, but certain design features hitherto associated with aesthetic or reform dress had begun to penetrate the most advanced Parisian couture houses." Valerie Steele, *The Corset: A Cultural History* (New Haven: Yale University Press, 2001), 146.
9   Discussing fashion promotion in films at this time, Charlotte Herzog says: "The commercial tie-ins and articles about stars and studio designers in fan magazines and local newspapers, along with the

narrative and dialogue of these feature films provided mutually supporting channels of exploitation." "'Powder Puff' Promotion: The Fashion Show-in-the-Film", in *Fabrications: Costume and the Female Body*, ed. Jane Gaines and Charlotte Herzog (New York: Routledge, 1990), 135.

10 Jane M. Gaines points out that another post-Code film, *Madam Satan* (dir. Cecil B. Demille, 1930), "presents us with a case where, although the narrative was found objectionable to censors, the solution to the problem of sexual representation was enforced at the level of the *mise-en-scène*. The narrative was not changed; instead, the costumes were modified." "On Wearing the Film: *Madam Satan* (1930)," in *Fashion Cultures: Theories, Explorations and Analysis*, ed. Stella Bruzzi and Pamela Church Gibson (New York: Routledge, 2000), 162.

11 Lucy Fischer, *Designing Women: Cinema, Art Deco, and the Female Form* (New York: Columbia University Press, 2003), 124.

12 Laura Mulvey, in *Fetishism and Curiosity*, examines film within the contexts of Marxist and Freudian theories of the fetish. She says the fetish "glitters": "it has to hold the fetishist's eyes fixed on the seduction of belief to guard against the encroachment of knowledge. This investment in surface appearance enhances the phantasmatic space of the fetish and sets up a structure in which object fixation can easily translate into image." (Bloomington: Indiana University Press, 1996), 6. The satin-clad woman's body contributes to this "guard against the encroachment of knowledge"—specifically, the glittering surface distracts viewers from awareness of the machinations of capitalist labor practices. For more on the fetish, see Chapter 4.

13 François Truffaut, "Lubitsch was a Prince," in *The Films in My Life* (Boston: Da Capo Press, 1994), 52.

14 For more on statuary and cinema, see *Screening Statues: Sculpture and Cinema*, ed. Steven Jacobs, Susan Felleman, Vito Adriaensens, and Lisa Colpaert (Edinburgh: Edinburgh University Press, 2017).

15 Lucy Fischer writes: "In its insistent contemporaneity, Art Deco was identified with the machine age—both in its imagery and its graphics. [...] Deco's attitude toward technology contrasts strongly with that

of its predecessor, Art Nouveau, which held sway from 1890 to 1914. That movement was highly identified with Nature as an oppositional stance to the Industrial Revolution." *Designing Women*, 12. Some other films in which satin and Art Deco style play important roles in costuming and décor: *Dinner at Eight* (dir. George Cukor, 1933); *Christopher Strong* (dir. Dorothy Arzner, 1933); *Shall We Dance* (dir. Mark Sandrich, 1937); and *The Palm Beach Story* (dir. Preston Sturges, 1942).

16 Fischer, *Designing Women*, 33.
17 Josephine Baker is an important exception. Baker's contributions to performance and costuming continue to be influential. See Alicja Sowinska, "Dialectic of the Banana Skirt: The Ambiguities of Josephine Baker's Self-Representation," *Michigan Feminist Studies* 19 (2005–6): 51–72.
18 Mary Ann Doane, *Femmes Fatales: Feminism, Film Theory, Psychoanalysis* (New York: Routledge, 1991), 142.
19 Ibid., 146.
20 Mick LaSalle, *Complicated Women: Sex and Power in Pre-Code Hollywood* (New York: St Martin's Press, 2000), 1.
21 Marketa Uhlirova, book review, *Screen* 60, no. 4 (Winter 2019): 637–41.
22 Esther Leslie, "Dreams for Sale," in *Birds of Paradise: Costume as Cinematic Spectacle*, ed. Marketa Uhlirova (London: Koenig Books, 2013), 31.
23 Kenneth Anger's 1965 short experimental film *Kustom Kar Kommandos* is also relevant to discussions of shine and longing. Matthew Tinkcom says that "*Kustom Kar Kommandos* commemorates the eroticized longing for the commodity that most of us *cannot* own, a longing most concentrated in the customizer's gaze on the brilliant surfaces that he polishes and admires." *Working Like a Homosexual: Camp, Capital, Cinema* (Durham: Duke University Press, 2002), 128–9. I discuss Anger's film *Puce Moment* in Chapter 5.
24 A special thank you to filmmaker and scholar Nina Fonoroff for her insights on this topic. See Chapter 2 for more on scattered lighting effects.

25 Victoria Z. Rivers, *The Shining Cloth: Dress and Adornment that Glitter* (New York: Thames & Hudson, 1999), 7–8.
26 Shiny coin-like objects on the film screen evoke Laura Mulvey's description of the image in capitalism: "the commodity presents the market with a seductive sheen." *Mulvey, Fetishism and Curiosity*, 4.
27 Theorist Georg Simmel speaks of the "radiating" quality attached to objects of adornment made from "shining metals and precious stones": "The radiations of adornment, the sensuous attention it provokes, supply the personality with such an enlargement or intensification of its sphere: the personality, so to speak, *is* more when it is adorned." Georg Simmel, 'Adornment', in Daniel Leonhard Pardy, ed., *The Rise of Fashion: A Reader* (Minneapolis: University of Minnesota Press, 2004), 81.
28 Karl Toepfer, "Dance, Fashion and Music Hall Scenes in European Silent Films of the 1920s," in *Birds of Paradise: Costume as Cinematic Spectacle*, ed. Marketa Uhlirova (London: Koenig Books, 2013), 245.
29 Ara Osterweil, "*Under the Skin*: The Perils of Becoming Female," *Film Quarterly* 67, no. 4 (2014), 44–51.
30 See Catherine Dormor's chapter "Textile as Viscous Substance" in her book *A Philosophy of Textile* (London: Bloomsbury, 2020). Dormor is largely concerned with contextualizing contemporary textile artists within French feminist thought, but her attention to the potential viscosity of fabric and to its material and structural qualities is also useful for conversations about the representation of textiles on film.

Chapter 2

1 For more about the environmental impact of synthetic fiber production, see Paul David Blanc, *Fake Silk: The Lethal History of Viscose Rayon* (New Haven: Yale University Press, 2016).
2 Pap Ndiaye, Nylon and Bombs : *Dupont and the March of Modern America*, trans. Elborg Forster (Baltimore: The Johns Hopkins Press,

2007), 2. For more on the chemical make-up of synthetic fabrics, see Walter Gratzer, *Giant Molecules: From Nylon to Nanotubes* (Oxford: Oxford University Press, 2009).

3   Rachel Worth, Fashion and Class (London: Bloomsbury, 2020), 122.

4   Ibid., 122.

5   Susannah Handley, *Nylon: The Story of a Fashion Revolution* (Baltimore: The Johns Hopkins University Press, 1999), 117.

6   Barbara Brownie and Danny Graydon write, on recent synthetics in exercise wear: "connotations of athleticism and physical performance have been reinforced, perhaps even strengthened, as sportswear has come to resemble superhero costumes increasingly over the past few decades." In *The Superhero Costume: Identity and Disguise in Fact and Fiction* (London: Bloomsbury, 2016), 44.

7   Handley, *Nylon: The Story of a Fashion Revolution*, 57.

8   For more on the history of globalization, see Ellen Rosen, *Making Sweatshops: The Globalization of the U.S. Apparel Industry* (Berkeley: University of California Press, 2002).

9   See the scholarship of Regina Blaszczyk for more on the impact of mass-produced synthetics on fashion and other areas.

10 Susan Smulyan, *Popular Ideologies: Mass Culture at Mid-Century* (Philadelphia: University of Pennsylvania Press, 2007), 42.

11 Elena Phipps, *Looking at Textiles: A Guide to Technical Terms* (Los Angeles: J. Paul Getty Museum, 2011), 33.

12 Giuliana Bruno, *Surface: Matters of Aesthetics, Materiality, and Media* (Chicago: University of Chicago Press, 2014), 36.

13 Esther Leslie, "Dreams for Sale," in *Birds of Paradise: Costume as Cinematic Spectacle*, ed. Marketa Uhlirova (London: Koenig Books, 2013), 34. Phyllis G. Tortora points out that celluloid-based yarns were in development during the nineteenth century, but did not enter the market as synthetic fabric until the twentieth century, adding that "the first true plastics synthesized from chemicals and not related to natural materials also appeared in the twentieth century." *Dress, Fashion, and Technology: From Prehistory to Present* (London: Bloomsbury, 2015), 132.

14 Mark Miodownik, *Stuff Matters* (New York: Houghton Mifflin Harcourt, 2014), 133. Miodownik adds that "the plastics that followed celluloid, such as Bakelite, nylon, vinyl, and silicone, built on its creative power and have also had an important impact on our cultural psyche. Bakelite became a moldable replacement for wood at a time when the telephone, radio, and television were being invented and needed a new material to embody their modernity. Nylon's sleekness took on the fashion industry, replaced silk as the material for women's stockings, and then spawned a new family of fabrics, such as Lycra and PVC, as well as a group of materials called elastomers, without which all our clothes would be baggy and our pants would fall down" (138).

15 Lou Taylor, "De-coding the Hierarchy of Fashion Textiles," in *The Textiles Reader*, ed. Jessica Hemmings (London: Bloomsbury, 2012), 421.

16 Walter Benjamin, "The Work of Art in the Age of Mechanical Reproduction" (1936), in *Illuminations*, trans. Harry Zohn (New York: Schocken Books, 1968), 239.

17 This viewpoint on polyester is indebted to the ideas established by Susan Sontag's essay "Notes on 'Camp,'" in *Against Interpretation and Other Essays* (New York: Dell Publishing, 1967).

18 Disco and polyester were on parallel trajectories of popularity and rejection in the 1970s. Disco, which is closely identified with polyester, experienced a significant backlash, culminating in 1979's Disco Demolition Night in Chicago. The association of disco with queer people of color underlines how the rage directed at this music and dance scene was also rooted in racism and homophobia.

19 Katy Kelleher, "From Victorians to Ravers: The Lustrous Magic of Iridescence in Fashion," *Jezebel*. September 8, 2020. https://theattic.jezebel.com/from-victorians-to-ravers-the-lustrous-magic-of-irides-1844752391.

20 The presentation of a feminized man in *Saturday Night Fever*, via the "look" of polyester, Tony's careful self-adornment, and the mood of nightclub lighting, poses questions about how we might read gender through aesthetics. In *Shimmering Images: Trans Cinema, Embodiment,*

and the Aesthetics of Change, Eliza Steinbock asks how aesthetics can reframe our understanding of difference: "What if trans embodiment is not primarily about sex or gender, but about experimenting with the aesthetics of corporeality in terms of efficacy and political purchase?" (Durham: Duke University Press, 2019), 6. While my focus on "shimmer" and gender expression is more literal and material-based than Steinbock's, their in-depth study extends the possibilities of how we might examine trans identity through cinematic analysis. See also the work of writer and curator Jeanne Vaccaro, whose work examines handcraft, aesthetics, and transgender studies.

21 Roland Barthes, *Mythologies*, trans. Annette Lavers (New York: Farrar, Straus and Giroux, 1972), 97–8. Katie Schaag echoes Barthes in celebrating the potential in plastic's changeability: "the inherent performativity of plasticity is located in its constitutive force—its power to reshape and reform itself continuously anew." Katie Schaag, "Biological Plasticity and Performative Possibility in the Work of Catherine Malabou and Curious," in *Inter Views in Performance Philosophy: Crossings and Conversations*, ed. Anna Street, Julien Alliot, and Magnolia Pauker (London: Palgrave Macmillan, 2017), 147.

22 Jack Halberstam, *Trans*: A Quick and Quirky Account of Gender Variability* (Berkeley: University of California Press, 2018), 154.

23 The binaries between "natural" and "unnatural," handmade and machine-made, are explored in *The Matrix* (dir. Wachowskis, 1999), which utilizes knit costuming in marked contrast to the constructed world of false synthetics. The plot of *The Matrix* depicts human bodies living in real and simulated realms. The "matrix" is what we think of as reality, but which in actuality is a simulation. The fabric of the team members' costuming helps us distinguish between spaces of "real" and "simulated" in the film. In the simulated world, the team wears synthetic, futuristic superhero-like wear suitable for action and athletic movement. After he has made his first appearance in reality, Neo awakens with a change in costume: he now wears a loose-knit sweater. The appearance of his ripped knit sweater contrasts starkly with the sleek synthetics of the matrix. Others in the team wear similar loose

knits, often ripped or frayed. While it is unclear whether these sweaters are made from synthetic or natural fibers, the use of worn-out, loosely pieced-together yarn suggests human making and wear, which helps establish this world as "real"—in other words, it is handmade, in use, and linked to the physical body.

24 Malcolm X, *The Autobiography of Malcolm X* (New York: Ballantine Books, 1964), 56.
25 See also the films of Jack Smith and the scholarship of Denilson Lopes.
26 Mike Kelley, "Cross Gender/Cross Genre," *PAJ: A Journal of Performance and Art* 22, no.1 (2000): 2. The 2011 Spanish film *The Skin I Live In*, directed by Pedro Almodóvar, explores connections among topics such as sexuality and artifice, skin and textile, surgery and identity. At the center of the film is plastic surgeon Dr. Robert Ledgard's invention of molded artificial flesh. A powerful Svengali figure, Dr. Ledgard uses surgical sewing and patching of synthetic skin to transform death into life and change men into women. His obsessive manipulation and "mending" of bodies is deemed illegal, and the synthetic skin takes on a criminal, subversive quality. The film's provocative linking of sewing with surgery, and skin with fabric, blurs boundaries among human skin, synthetic textiles, and film material, and intervenes in debates about medicine, chemistry, and gender expression. Almodóvar investigates the potentially liberating as well as oppressive possibilities in manipulated fake material. Much of the film's narrative involves questioning the meaning of "real" or "natural," especially in reference to gender. In developing story and characters who compel audiences to detach gender identity from bodies, Almodóvar forces us to consider the ethical consequences of rigidly defining what it is to be "male" or "female." For more about the film's treatment of fabric and the body, see Cath Davies, "What Lies Beneath: Fabric and Embodiment in Almodovar's *The Skin I Live In*," *Film, Fashion & Consumption* 6, no. 1 (2017): 66–79.
27 Live theater history also includes attempts to integrate smell, though this faded over time; Sally Banes writes: "Historically, the cultural uses of aromas in the West diminished with the hygiene campaigns of the

late 19th and early 20th centuries, since the spread of disease was linked to foul odors." "Olfactory Performances," *The Drama Review* 45, no. 1 (2001): 68.

28 Sianne Ngai, *Ugly Feelings* (Cambridge, MA: Harvard University Press, 2005), 332–3. Julia Kristeva's *Powers of Horror: An Essay on Abjection* (New York: Columbia University Press, 1982) provides another important theoretical foundation for reading Waters and abjection.

29 For more on Divine, see Michael Moon and Eve Kosofsky Sedgwick, "Divinity: A Dossier; A Performance Piece; A Little-Understood Emotion," *Discourse* 13, no. 1 (1990-1991): 12–39. Waters does not make trans identity an issue in *Polyester*. Because this is not a central concern of the film, Waters communicates an acceptance of Divine's identity and gender expression.

30 Julia Serano, *Whipping Girl: A Transexual Woman on Sexism and the Scapegoating of Femininity* (Berkeley: Seal Press, 2016), 5.

31 Paul B. Preciado, *Testo Junkie: Sex, Drugs, and Biopolitics in the Pharmacopornographic Era*, trans. Bruce Benderson (New York: Feminist Press, 2013), 32.

32 Arlen Austin, Beth Capper, and Tracey Deutsch, "Wages for Housework and Social Reproduction: A Microsyllabus," *Radical History Review*, April 27, 2020. https://www.radicalhistoryreview.org/abusablepast/wages-for-housework-and-social-reproduction-a-microsyllabus/.

33 Rozsika Parker, *The Subversive Stitch: Embroidery and the Making of the Feminine* (London: I.B. Tauris, 1984), 3.

34 Ibid., xix.

35 "Outside the 'high' art world, fiber gained a new visibility in the United States in the 1960s and 1970s with revivals of the traditional crafts of hand weaving, quilting, embroidery, dyeing, knotting and basketry. The social and artistic contexts and practices surrounding these revivals included the back-to-the-land and hippie movements, the renewed interest in folk art around the American Bicentennial, trends in the personalization of clothing like the adoption of African dress by African Americans, the feminist recuperation of women's history, the

revival of traditional arts of minority communities in the South and Southwest, and the popular craze of macramé." Elissa Auther, "Fiber Art and the Hierarchy of Art and Craft, 1960-1980," in *The Textiles Reader*, ed. Jessica Hemmings (London: Bloomsbury, 2012), 216.

36 Ibid., 218.
37 Interestingly, Anni Albers, who is often credited with raising the public status of weaving as an important, museum-worthy art form, referred to herself as "housewife" on her passport. An older generation than many of the 1970s feminist activists, Albers, despite her self-identification as a housewife, nonetheless was a central figure in bringing institutional and critical attention to the marginalized, feminized fiber arts.
38 Ibid., 217.
39 Anca Parvulescu, "Import/Export: Housework in an International Frame," *PMLA* 127, no. 4 (2012): 849.
40 Ivone Margulies, *Nothing Happens: Chantal Akerman's Hyperrealist Everyday* (Durham: Duke University Press, 1996), 69.

Chapter 3

1 Markings on fabric have a large and diverse history, and our perception of them often relies on cultural understanding. Our ability to discern printed messages depends on factors such as proximity, legibility, and cultural/linguistic knowledge. Prints communicate the wearer's taste and often their political and social affiliations. An important aspect of communicating via textiles is what is conveyed on the surface of the fabric: viewers can reliably understand recognizable prints. Many prints—examples include Scottish plaids or Navajo designs—are helpful in conveying cultural associations and historical trends. For filmmakers, the instant familiarity of certain designs assists in character development by communicating identity quickly and directly. Recontextualized on screen, prints change meaning as they are projected across space and time.

2. Michel Pastoureau, *The Devil's Cloth: A History of Stripes and Striped Fabric*, trans. Jody Gladding (New York: Columbia University Press, 1991), 22. See also Jude Stewart, *Patternalia: An Unconventional History of Polka Dots, Stripes, Plaid, Camouflage, & Other Graphic Patterns* (London: Bloomsbury, 2015). Sadie Plant points out: "stripes and checks are among the most basic of colored and textured designs which can be woven in. Both are implicit in the grids of the woven cloth itself." *Zeros + Ones* (London: Fourth Estate Limited, 1997), 66.

3. Several patterned textiles have traveled through the cinematic medium and emerged altered. In Western cultures, the presentation of Kente cloth and wax print fabrics on film has contributed significantly to the erasure of textile histories from individual countries and cultures in Africa. Film costumers often merge diverse textile histories, problematically, into one fantasized "African textile." Yinka Shonibare has called wax resist cloth, a textile with its own complex pre- and post-colonial histories, a signifier of "Africanness." Kente cloth, too, is a useful example of how print can take on multiple meanings as it passes through temporal and spatial movement, as well as the motion of media imagery. Both wax print fabrics and Kente cloth have, due in part to their portrayal on film, been central in discourse about textiles and the representation of a generalized "African" identity. One example appears in the 1988 film *Coming to America* (dir. John Landis), about a fantasized country in Africa (Zamunda). The film employs Dutch wax print throughout in order to identify the main characters as African and to explore the African-American characters' perception of real (or imagined) Africa. *Coming to America*, a mainstream Hollywood comedy, does not pretend to portray Zamunda in a realistic manner. But it does rely on costuming to tell the story of the characters' movement from Africa to New York, and to continuously call attention to the way their clothing visually contrasts with that of their largely African American community in Queens. At the same time as they may produce a reductionist version of national identity, some films have used cinematic display of textiles in ways that give audiences a tool for political expression extending beyond the theatrical setting.

Fabrics featuring distinctly African (or African-looking) prints was central in building cultural self-identification and empowerment—the dissemination of images of African-Americans wearing "African" textiles (usually wax print or Kente cloth) on television and in films and photographs in the late 1960s and early 1970s created an association of the printed fabrics with counterculture and political struggle. The reappropriation of Kente cloth and various wax prints within African-American political movement has given new context to these patterns; "African" fabrics have been refigured on screen in order to strengthen feelings of cultural belonging and political solidarity among African-American audiences. As an important recent example, *Black Panther* (2018, dir. Ryan Coogler) portrays the powerful fictional African country of Wakanda. Utilizing futuristic, highly stylized costumes incorporating traditional printed textiles from African cultures, *Black Panther* offers an empowering approach to the on-screen portrayal of printed textiles and their role in the global movement of meaning and imagery.

4 The 1966 William Klein film *Who are You, Polly Magoo?* makes significant use of black-and-white striping to create contrast and dramatic effect. The film is a satire of 1960s designers such as Rudi Gernreich who used unusual materials in their clothing—it opens with a fashion show that includes garments made of large aluminum sheets, a parody of the unwearability of some avant-garde designs (one model in the film slashes her arm with the metal clothing). Among the most striking images from this film are those that capture the highly stylized use of black-and-white striping. A scene in which models are photographed applying makeup has become the still most often associated with the film. The stripes-on-stripes patterning extends from the models to the walls to the black-and-white cinematography. The scene is choreographed and posed (later we learn this was a session for a magazine photograph). The layers of artifice and theatricality present in the scene—as the models apply makeup and mirror each other—are heightened by the bold, unnatural-looking use of stripes.

5 Juliet Ash, *Dress Behind Bars: Prison Clothing as Criminality* (London: I.B. Tauris, 2009), 67.
6 Ibid., 39. Ash states: "Not only were prison uniforms designed to prevent escape but they were also fashioned to humiliate the wearer. As prisoners have indicated in their writings, prison clothing marked out convicts as risible or to be pitied in the eyes of the public. This first uniform that embodied punishment was an integral part of an increasingly surveillant prison culture in America in the first half of the nineteenth century." (25) In addition, Ash writes, regarding the symbolism of black-and-white striped fabric, "the black-and-white horizontal stripes symbolically represented prison bars that not only surrounded the inmate but were also imprinted on the convict's body and thus became an embodiment of imprisonment." (25)
7 Caroline Evans, "Yesterday's Emblems and Tomorrow's Commodities: The Return of the Repressed in Fashion Imagery Today," in *Fashion Cultures: Theories, Explorations and Analysis*, ed. Stella Bruzzi and Pamela Church Gibson (New York: Routledge, 2000), 100.
8 Beverly Gordon, *Textiles: The Whole Story* (London: Thames and Hudson, 2011), 181–2.
9 The word "print" itself refers to a type of visual communication or written language. Like language, patterned fabric can change within different contexts, is usually culturally specific, and utilizes the power of repetition.
10 For more on narrative and symbolism in *Black Girl* see Jonathon Repinecz, "'This is Not a Pipe'?: Reflexivity, Fictionality, and Diologism in Sembène's Films," *Journal of African Cinemas* 8, no. 2 (2016): 181–97.
11 Sembène is often cited as the first filmmaker from post-colonial Africa. He was part of the international aesthetic movements of the 1960s and 1970s (such as "Third Cinema") that framed the medium of film and the work of filmmaking in the context of political struggle for independence.
12 Rachael Langford, "Black and White in Black and White Identity and Cinematography in Ousmane Sembène's *La Noire de . . . /Black Girl* (1966)," *Studies in French Cinema* 1, no.1 (2001): 13.

13 Ibid., 16.
14 Frantz Fanon writes of the white gaze on the black body: "all around the body reigns an atmosphere of certain uncertainty." *Black Skin, White Masks*, trans. Richard Philcox (New York: Grove Press, 2008), 90.
15 Karen Tranberg Hansen, "Introduction," in *African Dress: Fashion, Agency, Performance*, ed. Karen Tranberg Hansen and D. Soyini Madison (London: Bloomsbury, 2013), 2.
16 Diouana's mental decline and distress in the Antibes apartment recalls Frantz Fanon's statement that a black man traveling in Europe is "made to feel inferior." From *Black Skin, White Masks* (1952), trans. Richard Philcox (New York: Grove Press, 2008), 127.
17 Leslie W. Rabine, *The Global Circulation of African Fashion* (Oxford: Berg, 2002), 28.
18 Adam Geczy, *Fashion and Orientalism: Dress, Textiles, and Culture from the 17th to the 21st Century* (London: Bloomsbury, 2013), 151.
19 Mick LaSalle, *Complicated Women: Sex and Power in Pre-Code Hollywood* (New York: St Martin's Press, 2000), 41–2.
20 Dick Hebdige, *Subculture: The Meaning of Style* (London: Routledge, 1979), 2.
21 Wayne Koestenbaum, *Humiliation* (New York: Picador, 2011), 100.
22 Janey Place and Lowell Peterson, "Some Visual Motifs of Film Noir," in *Film Noir Reader*, ed. Alain Silver and James Ursini (New York: Limelight, 1996), 66.
23 Stella Bruzzi, *Undressing Cinema: Clothing and Identity in the Movies* (London: Routledge, 1997), 126.
24 Robert J. Corber, "Joan Crawford's Padded Shoulders: Female Masculinity in *Mildred Pierce*," *Camera Obscura* 21, no. 2 (2006): 24.

Chapter 4

1 The film industry has often, for marketing purposes, used 3D and other technological effects to suggest a closer spatial relationship between viewer and screen.

2   Textile wall-hangings and tapestries could also be included in the category of untouchable art objects.
3   Jennifer M. Barker, *The Tactile Eye: Touch and the Cinematic Experience* (Berkeley: University of California Press, 2009), 32. See also the work of Eva Hayward in regards to tactility and the animal, for example in "Fingeryeyes: Impressions of Cup Corals," *Cultural Anthropology*, 25, no. 4 (November 2010): 577–99.
4   Pennina Barnett, "Folds, Fragments, Surfaces: Towards a Poetics of Cloth," in *The Textile Reader*, ed. Jessica Hemmings (London: Bloomsbury, 2012), 185.
5   Laura McMahon, Cinema and Contact : *The Withdrawal of Touch in Nancy, Bresson, Duras, and Denis* (New York: Routledge, 2012), 43.
6   Sarah Montross, "Screens: Virtual Material," in *Introduction to Screens: Virtual Material* (Lincoln, MA: deCordova Sculpture Park and Museum, 2017), 11.
7   Often the interactions among bodies, props, and settings in the screen space combine to create meaning. Referring specifically to the usefulness of phenomenology in queer studies, Sara Ahmed writes of "the importance of lived experience, the intentionality of consciousness, the significance of nearness or what is ready-to-hand, and the role of repeated and habitual actions in shaping bodies and worlds." These principles, and especially "the significance of nearness" complicate perceptions of textiles within cinematic mise-en-scène. Ahmed's in-depth look at "orientation," the relationship between bodies and non-human objects, and sexuality provides me with an underlying theoretical viewpoint in order to consider the role of textiles in on-screen spatial dynamics. Camera distance and the relative closeness of actor and fabric change seemingly mundane "repeated and habitual actions" into meaningful commentary. Sara Ahmed, *Queer Phenomenology: Orientations, Objects, Others* (Durham: Duke University Press, 2007), 2.
8   Laura U. Marks, *The Skin of the Film: Intercultural Cinema, Embodiment, and the Senses* (Durham: Duke University Press, 2000), 183.

9   Leopold von Sacher-Masoch, "Venus in Furs," in *Masochism*, trans. Jean McNeil (New York: Zone Books, 1991), 177.
10 Sigmund Freud, "The Sexual Aberrations' (1905)," in *Three Essays on the Theory of Sexuality*, trans. James Strachey (New York: Basic Books, 2000), 19.
11 Walter Benjamin, *The Arcades Project*, trans. Howard Eiland and Kevin McLaughlin (Cambridge, MA: Harvard University Press, 1999), 69.
12 Ulrich Lehmann, "Benjamin and the Revolution of Fashion" (2000), in *Fashion Theory: A Reader*, ed. Malcolm Barnard (New York: Routledge, 2007), 433.
13 Alexandra Shulman, *Clothes . . . and other things that matter* (London: Cassell, 2020), 286.
14 Elena Phipps, *Looking at Textiles: A Guide to Technical Terms* (Los Angeles: J. Paul Getty Museum, 2011) 58.
15 Anne Hamlyn writes, "like a sumptuous textile, cinema has been seen as a seductive, fetishized and fetishizing, surface that both is, and is not, what it represents or enfolds." Anne Hamlyn, "Freud, Fabric, Fetish," in *The Textile Reader*, ed. Jessica Hemmings (London: Bloomsbury, 2012), 16.
16 Charles Drazin, *Charles Drazin on Blue Velvet* (London: Bloomsbury, 1998), 14.
17 Scholars have investigated subjects such as psychoanalytic motivation, taboo, criminality, mother-longing, and homosexuality in *Blue Velvet*. For more on dress in David Lynch's work, see Lynda Chapple, "In Threads and Tatters: Costume, Identification and Female Subjectivity in *Mulholland Dr*," *Cultural Studies Review* 17, no. 1 (2011): 320–38.
18 "Vallens" sounds like "valance," a type of decorative curtaining.
19 Robert Stoller, *Observing the Erotic Imagination* (New Haven: Yale University Press, 1985), 155.
20 Hamlyn, "Freud, Fabric, Fetish," 19.
21 Ibid., 17.
22 Ibid., 18.
23 Alice A. Kuzniar, "Ears Looking at You: E.T.A. Hoffman's *The Sandman* and David Lynch's *Blue Velvet*," *South Atlantic Review* 54, no. 2 (1989): 7.

24 Paul Whittaker and Clio Padovani, "Testing, Orthodoxy: Collecting, The Gaze, Knitting the Impossible," in *The Textile Reader*, ed. Jessica Hemmings (London: Bloomsbury, 2012), 175.
25 Walter Murch, *In the Blink of an Eye: A Perspective on Film Editing*, 2nd ed. (Los Angeles: Silman-James Press, 2001), 57.
26 Scissors as a threatening weapon is used in Jean-Luc Godard's 1965 *Pierrot le Fou*. See also avant-garde performance and video art, for example Yoko Ono's performance *Cut Piece* (1964) and Paul Sharits's film *T,O,U,C,H,I,N,G* (1968).
27 Though not my primary concern here, the concept of "suture theory" in film studies is relevant to this discussion of editing and to my interest in linking filmmaking with textile-making. Elsaesser and Hagener write of suture theory: "The moment of rupture introduced by editing potentially brings the otherwise hidden machinery of vision (the 'apparatus') to the viewer's attention, and thus produces a moment of anxiety and loss, which the subsequent shot has to retrieve, bind up, or stitch together, in short—has to *suture*." Thomas Elsaesser and Malte Hagener, *Film Theory: An Introduction Through the Senses*, 2nd ed. (New York: Routledge, 2015), 102. See also Catherine Dormor's chapter "Seaming" in her book *A Philosophy of Textile* (London: Bloomsbury, 2020).
28 David Copenhafer, "Mourning and Music in *Blue Velvet*," *Camera Obscura* 23, no. 3 (2008): 137.
29 Barker, *The Tactile Eye*, 38.
30 In *Sherlock Jr.* (dir. Buster Keaton, 1924), the dreaming film projectionist walks through the film screen in order to enact his romantic fantasies and take charge of his everyday reality. The moment he transcends the physical boundary dividing film life from real life is surprising and magical. Similarly, in *The Purple Rose of Cairo* (dir. Woody Allen, 1985), a Depression-era woman finds excitement and romance as her on-screen love interest notices her and emerges from the film into the theater in order to meet her in real life. The act of walking though the film screen is a temporary moment of transcendence in which projected image meets reality and longing

is satisfied. For more on silent film audience's relationship with the screen, see Wanda Strauven, "Early Cinema's Touch(able) Screens: From Uncle Josh to Ali Barbouyou," *European Journal of Media Studies* 1, no. 2 (2012): 155–76.

31 Marks, *The Skin of the Film*, 192.
32 Ibid., 187.
33 Roland Barthes's question, "Is not the most erotic portion of a body where the garment gapes?" is relevant here. Associated with visual erotic interplay between fabric and skin, moving textiles and curtains produce an effect similar to a "gape"—the place where skin is revealed, partially obstructed by fabric—in a garment. Roland Barthes, *The Pleasure of the Text*, trans. Richard Miller (New York: Farrar, Straus and Giroux, 1975), 9.
34 Sarah Gilligan, "Heaving Cleavages and Fantastic Frock Coats: Gender Fluidity, Celebrity and Tactile Transmediality in Contemporary Costume Cinema," *Film, Fashion & Consumption* 1, no. 1 (2012): 26.
35 For more on the cheongsam see Cheryl Sim, *Wearing the Cheongsam: Dress and Culture in a Chinese Diaspora* (London: Bloomsbury, 2019).
36 Liz Rideal, "The Echoes of Erotic Cloth in Film," in *The Erotic Cloth: Seduction and Fetishism in Textiles*, ed. Lesley Millar and Alice Kettle (London: Bloomsbury, 2018), 153.
37 Giuliana Bruno, *Surface: Matters of Aesthetics, Materiality, and Media* (Chicago: University of Chicago Press, 2014), 29.
38 Gilles Deleuze, *The Fold: Leibniz and the Baroque*, transl. Tom Conley (Minneapolis: University of Minnesota Press, 1993), 34.
39 The material, detached from character, also produces its own affect. As Eugenie Brinkema explains, this focus on exteriority "is no longer the expression of an interior state or property of the classical subject but an affective exteriority, an ectoaffect—a formal affectivity of shape, structure, duration, line light." Brinkema's emphasis on the interrelation of form and affect offers a method for reading materiality, form, and emotion simultaneously. This perspective is especially useful in interpreting the textures, structures, and light-reflecting qualities of fabric on film. Eugenie Brinkema, *The Forms of the Affects* (Durham: Duke University Press, 2014), 23.

40 Gen Doy, *Drapery: Classicism and Barbarism in Visual Culture* (London: I.B. Tauris, 2002), 99. The quoted text is taken from a passage about Freud, fetishism, and drapery.
41 Sheer fabric, like the privacy curtain in *It Happened One Night*, plays on the concealing/revealing aspect of erotic expression. Two films, *The Cheat* (dir. Cecil B. DeMille, 1918) and *Shanghai Express* (dir. Josef von Sternberg, 1932) make interesting use of "sheerness" in exploring xenophobia and taboo. These two films use transparent or near-transparent material to create a mood of anxiety: a fear of touching the "other" and also a fear of being seen as criminal and/or sexually subversive. In illuminating the triangular relationship among fabric, touch, and otherness, the films depict making contact as simultaneously violent and titillating.

Chapter 5

1 Rebecca Solnit, *River of Shadows: Eadweard Muybridge and the Technological Wild West* (New York: Penguin, 2003), 4.
2 *The Assassin* (dir. Hou Hsiao-Hsien, 2015) includes a helpful example of how moving film works with fabrics in motion to create a sense of suspense. Yinniang, the assassin, carries out several of her acts of vengeance as a kind of phantom-voyeur. Set in ninth century China, the film follows Yinniang as she grapples with the ethical consequences of her assassination assignments. Seen by the film viewer but unnoticed by those she pursues, Yinniang is a watching presence who seeks cover as she stalks her prey. In one scene Yinniang is, unknown to her target, inside his home and lurking behind rows of interior hanging curtains. The camera moves through and around the setting. At the start of this scene we are firmly in Yinniang's point of view, watching behind filmy, sheer fabric and wondering if she will be caught spying. When she is revealed, we switch perspectives and assume the position of her target. The movement of the camera allows the viewer to have a three-dimensional experience, giving us access to both points of view. With

each decision made about the placement of the camera in the space between and around the hanging fabric and the later editing of these shots, the filmmakers are determining how much the audience is aware of what is happening on screen.

3   Catherine Hindson, "Dancing on Top of the World: A Serpentine through Late Nineteenth-Century Entertainment, Fashion, and Film," in *Birds of Paradise: Costume as Cinematic Spectacle*, ed. Marketa Uhlirova (London: Koenig Books, 2013), 66.

4   Filmmakers also use fabric in motion to express joy, ecstasy, and celebration. For example, in *Mahogany* (1975, dir. Berry Gordy), the protagonist, an aspiring fashion designer, tosses fabric in the air in a scene to mark the happiness that accompanies her rapidly accelerating career success.

5   Liz Rideal, 'The Echoes of Erotic Cloth in Film,' in *The Erotic Cloth: Seduction and Fetishism in Textiles*, ed. Alice Kettle and Lesley Millar (London: Bloomsbury, 2018), 149.

6   As they highlight our desire to see what is beyond the limits of the screen, moving textiles can develop viewpoints that simultaneously romanticize and degrade cultural difference. Films such as the mainstream Hollywood film *The Sheik* (1921), a financially successful, influential film whose messages about fear, colonization, travel, and cultural difference continue to be echoed in more contemporary depictions of the Middle East on film, uses curtains to develop a dreamlike mise-en-scène. *The Sheik* is a Rudolph Valentino vehicle in which Valentino stars as Ahmed, a sheik who abducts Diana, a wealthy English woman, and eventually wins her love. This film is not subtle in its portrayal of a simultaneously eroticized and villainized Middle Eastern desert community. Curtaining helps create the sense that we are peering into an exoticized world of The Other: a mysterious, dangerous East. The settings of *The Sheik* reinforce the colonialist's fantasy of the region, and the film's camera techniques emphasize that we are watching the colonialist's perspective into an "other" world. The film sets up framing devices, both in the camera (in the use of an iris) and in the mise-en-scène (in the use of curtains, walls, and doorways)

that provide us with a voyeur's perspective. At the beginning of the film, Diana, who has been established as a free-thinking middle to upper-class white woman, set her mind to penetrating an "Arabs-only" space. Disguising herself in local dress, Diana slips into private rooms only to be discovered by the sheik himself, who is merely amused by her outrageous sense of entitlement. In this "playful" recreation of colonialist invasion, Diana is imagined as a curious and harmless young woman. Her bold innocence is seductive to the sheik. Diana is first visited by the sheik in her bedroom at night, when he goes into her room via an open window—she sleeps in a bed surrounded by drapery that flutters in the wind. Later, Diana is kidnapped by the sheik and kept in a series of connected tents. The hanging fabrics of the tents suggest endless rooms and spatial depth in what is in reality most likely a shallow stage set. Often the sides of the screen are darkened, giving us a limited point of view and suggesting mysterious goings-on beyond the frame. Moving curtains also produce a kind of dissolve effect, indicating what feels like a temporal and spatial transition into a romanticized, "exotic" past.

7 Historically, on film, the intersection of wind and eroticism is found in the often comic and titillating examples of wind blowing women's clothing. The iconic example is the moment Marilyn Monroe's skirt is lifted over a subway grate in the 1955 film *The Seven-Year Itch* (dir. Billy Wilder). Half a century earlier, the silent Edison film *What Happened on Twenty-Third Street, New York City* (1901) documents a woman surprised by the skirt-raising air emerging from a sidewalk subway grate.

8 Kevin L. Ferguson, "Painting in the Dark: The Ambivalence of Air in Cinema," *Camera Obscura* 26, no. 2 (2011): 35–6. See also: Saige Walton and Nadine Boljkovac, "Introduction: Materialising Absence," *Screening the Past*, no. 43 (2018): 1–6.

9 Gilles Deleuze, *The Fold: Leibniz and the Baroque*, trans. Tom Conley (Minneapolis: University of Minnesota Press, 1993), 31.

10 *Air and Dreams: An Essay on the Imagination of Movement*, trans. Edith R. Farrell and C. Frederick Farrell (Dallas: The Dallas Institute of Humanities and Culture, 1988), 230.

11 See also *The Wind* (dir. Victor Sjöström, 1928).
12 See Mary Ann Doane, *The Desire to Desire: The Woman's Film of the 1940s* (Bloomington: Indiana University Press, 1987).
13 As Hitchcock's focus is often on the development of suspense, curtains come up repeatedly in his films; a noteworthy example is the famous shower curtain scene in his 1960 film *Psycho*.
14 My readings rely largely on scholarship done in textile/dress studies and media studies; however, growing research examining interior design and architecture on film also informs my work. Examples include Jean Whitehead's *Creating Interior Atmosphere: Mise-en-scène and Interior Design* (London: Bloomsbury, 2017) and Alexa Griffith Winton's chapter "Framing Interiority: Film Sets and the Discipline of Interior Design," in *Interiors Beyond Architecture*, ed. Deborah Schneiderman and Amy Campos (New York: Routledge, 2018).
15 Catherine Dormor, *A Philosophy of Textile: Between Practice and Theory* (London: Bloomsbury, 2020), 83.
16 David Lynch and Peter Greenaway are examples of two filmmakers who have incorporated the theatrical tradition of curtaining in noteworthy ways into the cinematic medium.
17 Pennina Barnett, "Folds, Fragments, Surfaces: Towards a Poetics of Cloth," in *The Textile Reader*, ed. Jessica Hemmings (London: Bloomsbury, 2012), 184. On the parallels between film and the baroque period of art, Saige Walton writes: "In the skin-deep sensibility of the baroque, the material make-up of worldly phenomena as well as subjective states of feeling will be made visible, sensible, and texturally available." *Cinema's Baroque Flesh: Film, Phenomenology and the Art of Entanglement* (Amsterdam: Amsterdam University Press, 2016) 167.
18 Thomas Elsaesser and Malte Hagener, *Film Theory: An Introduction Through the Senses*, 2nd ed. (New York: Routledge, 2015), 41.
19 Açalya Allmer, "In-between Stage Life and Everyday Life: Curtains and their Pictorial Representations," *Textile: The Journal of Cloth and Culture* 6 no. 1 (2008): 22.
20 The Structuralist film movement, which explored the mechanics of film and perception as well as the material relationship between film

and viewer, is an important touchstone for considering audience, technology, and fabric.

21 Much of filmmaker Jack Smith's work is characterized by dense ornamentation and richly draped surfaces. In his 1964 experimental film *Normal Love*, Smith eschews narrative clarity for maximalist settings and campy Orientalism. Enhanced by film techniques that jump, shake, and reveal imperfection, *Normal Love* builds up a pulsating, glittering film screen. Its impact can be seen in contemporary films such as *Madame Satã* (2002, dir. Karim Aïnouz). For more on Brazilian cinema, gender, and ornamentation, see the published scholarship of Denilson Lopes.

22 For more on decadence and experimental film, see Carel Rowe, *The Baudelairean Cinema: A Trend Within the American Avant-Garde* (Ann Arbor: University of Michigan Press, 1982).

23 Matthew Tinkcom, *Working Like a Homosexual: Camp, Capital, Cinema* (Durham: Duke University Press, 2002), 127. See Juan A. Suárez, "Kenneth Anger: Clothing, Queerness, Magic," in *Birds of Paradise: Costume as Cinematic Spectacle*, ed. Marketa Uhlirova (London: Koenig Books, 2013).

24 Gen Doy, *Drapery: Classicism and Barbarism in Visual Culture* (London: I.B. Tauris, 2002), 61.

25 The origins of film camera filters are linked to the use of fabric as a sort of "curtain" hung over the lens, and this use of filmy fabrics in cinematography is echoed in curtain props in front of the camera. Kenneth Anger would likely appreciate the following story, quoted from silent movie actress Colleen Moore. In her autobiography, Moore says that technological innovation in filtering began as an attempt to make older actresses appear younger during the production of D. W. Griffith's *Broken Blossoms* in 1919. Moore writes: "When the picture was released, we all rushed to see it. What we'd heard was true. Lillian Gish looked astonishingly young. Finally Mr. Griffith let everyone in on the secret. Billy Bitzer had covered his camera lens with black maline, a fine, silk net, the small holes in the material acting as a retouching lens. From then on, cameramen went berserk. They made test after test, not

only with black net, but with pink net, blue net, and, for blondes, gold net. They even tried layers of net, until the faces of some stars were so fuzzy it was hard to tell who they were. Out of all this experimentation came the diffusion lens. Some of the early ones were made with circles in the glass to break up the light. Others were a crosshatch of fine lines. Eventually they became so refined that today actresses in their fifties photograph like glamour girls." Colleen Moore, *Silent Star* (New York: Doubleday & Co, Inc., 1968) 35.

Conclusion

1 "Fabric in Film and Film as Fabric: Maya Deren's *Meshes of the Afternoon*," *Textile: The Journal of Cloth and Culture* 8, no. 2 (2010): 226–41.
2 In September of 2018, *Posthaste Perennial Pattern* was projected on the giant screens of New York City's Times Square. Showing the film across multiple screens reflects the frenzied visual imagery of Times Square itself, while also serving as a meditation on how everyday life presents us with a constant stream of prints and patterns. The placement of *Posthaste Perennial Pattern* in Times Square reinforces how visual pattern, abstraction, and movement characterize much of our daily visual experience. The speed of the editing in the film reflects the fast-moving images of contemporary life, where our eyes take in information quickly, often merely registering a piece of a larger pattern.
3 Uncovering information about making is closely connected to the archiving of historically significant textiles. The physicality of these materials, and especially the effects of decay, is concerning, and presents challenges for both film and textile preservationists. Pennina Barnett tells us, "this is a space of surface and texture, material and matter: the physical stuff from which things are made. Of cloth that sags, and linen that wears, and acrylic that washes through warp and through weft. Of gesso that cracks like sun-bleached earth; transformed from ground in days of old, to surface and subject that starts to speak

of closeness and distance, and inside and out." Pennina Barnett, "Folds, Fragments, Surfaces: Towards a Poetics of Cloth," in *The Textile Reader*, ed. Jessica Hemmings (London: Bloomsbury, 2012), 185. The specific impact of physical decay of the film strip is explored in Bill Morrison's films *Decasia* (2002) and *Dawson City: Frozen Time* (2016).

4 Twentieth century avant-garde film movements have a tradition of making the means of production visible to audiences.

5 In small productions, the film director is often also the cinematographer and editor. Working outside of the large Hollywood studios, small-budget filmmakers tend to deal with different systems of money flow and production. As the film industry expands into a digital media industry, looking to avant-garde film history is essential to maintaining an awareness of labor and materiality. Experimental film operates in opposition to the mass production of mainstream Hollywood by exposing and critiquing the exploitative nature of the industry and at the same time innovating within the craft of filmmaking.

6 For more on the influence of coding and the digital on fashion, textiles, and fabric-based art, see Sarah E. Braddock Clarke and Jane Harris, *Digital Visions for Fashion and Textiles: Made in Code* (New York: Thames & Hudson, 2012).

7 Publications on this topic include: Tilak Dias, *Electronic Textiles: Smart Fabric and Wearable Technology* (Cambridge: Woodhead Publishing, 2015); J. McCann and D. Bryson, *Smart Clothes and Wearable Technology* (Cambridge: Woodhead Publishing, 2009); Nithikul Nimkulrat, Faith Kane, and Kerry Walton, eds., *Crafting Textiles in the Digital Age* (London: Bloomsbury, 2016), Bradley Quinn, *Textile Futures: Fashion, Design, and Technology* (London: Berg, 2010).

8 See Nimkulrat, Kane, and Walton, *Crafting Textiles in the Digital Age*.

9 Sadie Plant, *Zeros + Ones* (London: Fourth Estate Limited, 1997), 69.

10 Giuliana Bruno, *Surface: Matters of Aesthetics, Materiality, and Media* (Chicago: University of Chicago Press, 2014), 7–8.

Bibliography

Adamson, Glenn. *Thinking Through Craft*. London: Bloomsbury, 2007.
Adamson, Glenn, ed. *The Craft Reader*. London: Bloomsbury, 2010.
Adamson, Glenn. *The Invention of Craft*. London: Bloomsbury, 2013.
Adamson, Glenn and Victoria Kelley, eds. *Surface Tensions: Surface, Finish, and the Meaning of Objects*. Manchester: Manchester University Press, 2013.
Ahmed, Sara. *Queer Phenomenology: Orientations, Objects, Others*. Durham: Duke University Press, 2007.
Albers, Anni. *On Weaving*. Princeton: Princeton University Press, 2017.
Allmer, Açalya. "In-between Stage Life and Everyday Life: Curtains and Their Pictorial Representations." *Textile: The Journal of Cloth and Culture* 6, no. 1 (2008): 18–31.
Andrew, Dudley. "The Neglected Tradition of Phenomenology in Film Theory." In *Movies and Methods, Volume 2*, edited by Bill Nichols, 625–32. Berkeley: University of California Press, 1985.
Ash, Juliet. *Dress Behind Bars: Prison Clothing as Criminality*. London: I.B. Tauris, 2009.
Auther, Elissa. *String Felt Thread: The Hierarchy of Art and Craft in American Art*. Minneapolis: University of Minnesota Press, 2010.
Auther, Elissa. "Fiber Art and the Hierarchy of Art and Craft, 1960-1980." In *The Textiles Reader*, edited by Jessica Hemmings, 210–22. London: Bloomsbury, 2012.
Bachelard, Gaston. *Air and Dreams: An Essay on the Imagination of Movement*, translated by Edith R. Farrell and C. Frederick Farrell. Dallas: The Dallas Institute of Humanities and Culture, 1988.
Bancroft, Alison. *Fashion and Psychoanalysis*. London: I.B. Tauris, 2012.
Banes, Sally. "Olfactory Performances." *The Drama Review* 45, no. 1 (2001): 68–76.

Barber, Elizabeth Wayland. *Women's Work: The First 20,000 Years*. New York: W.W. Norton, 1994.

Barker, Jennifer M. *The Tactile Eye: Touch and the Cinematic Experience*. Berkeley: University of California Press, 2009.

Barnard, Malcolm, ed. *Fashion Theory: A Reader*. London: Routledge, 2007.

Barnes, Ruth and Joanne B. Eicher, eds. *Dress and Gender: Making and Meaning*. Oxford: Berg, 1992.

Barnett, Pennina. "Folds, Fragments, Surfaces: Towards a Poetics of Cloth." In *The Textile Reader*, edited by Jessica Hemmings, 182–90. London: Bloomsbury, 2012.

Barthes, Roland. *Mythologies*, translated by Annette Lavers. New York: Farrar, Straus and Giroux, 1972.

Barthes, Roland. *The Pleasure of the Text*, translated by Richard Miller. New York: Farrar, Straus and Giroux, 1975.

Barthes, Roland. *The Fashion System*, translated by Ward and Howard. Berkeley: University of California Press, 1983.

Barthes, Roland. *The Language of Fashion*, translated by Andy Stafford. London: Bloomsbury, 2013.

Baudrillard, Jean. *Simulacra and Simulation*, translated by Sheila Faria Glaser. Ann Arbor: The University of Michigan Press, 1994.

Baudrillard, Jean. *The System of Objects*, translated by James Benedict. New York: Verso, 1996.

Beckert, Sven. *Empire of Cotton: A Global History*. New York: Penguin Random House, 2014.

Ben-Horin, Karen, ed. *The Sweater: A History*. Atglen, PA: Schiffer Publishing, 2017.

Benjamin, Walter. *Illuminations*, translated by Harry Zohn. New York: Schocken Books, 1968.

Benjamin, Walter. *Reflections*, translated by Edmund Jephcott. New York: Schocken Books, 1986.

Benjamin, Walter. *The Arcades Project*, translated by Howard Eiland and Kevin McLaughlin. Cambridge, MA: Harvard University Press, 1999.

Bergstrom, Janet and Mary Ann Doane, eds. "*The Spectatrix*" (special issue). *Camera Obscura* 7, no. 2–3 (1989).

Blanc, Paul David. *Fake Silk: The Lethal History of Viscose Rayon*. New Haven: Yale University Press, 2016.
Brinkema, Eugenie. *The Forms of the Affects*. Durham: Duke University Press, 2014.
Brownie, Barbara and Danny Graydon. *The Superhero Costume: Identity and Disguise in Fact and Fiction*. London: Bloomsbury, 2016.
Bruno, Giuliana. *Surface: Matters of Aesthetics, Materiality, and Media*. Chicago: University of Chicago Press, 2014.
Bruzzi, Stella. *Undressing Cinema: Clothing and Identity in the Movies*. London: Routledge, 1997.
Bruzzi, Stella and Pamela Church Gibson, eds. *Fashion Cultures: Theories, Explorations and Analysis*. New York: Routledge, 2000.
Cavallaro, Dani and Alexandra Warwick, eds. *Fashioning the Frame: Boundaries, Dress and Body*. Oxford: Berg, 1998.
Chapple, Lynda. "In Threads and Tatters: Costume, Identification and Female Subjectivity in *Mulholland Dr*." *Cultural Studies Review* 17, no. 1 (2011): 320–38.
Clark, Judith. "Statement VI." In *The Textiles Reader*, edited by Jessica Hemmings, 191–7. London: Bloomsbury, 2012.
Clarke, Sarah E. Braddock and Jane Harris, eds. *Digital Visions for Fashion and Textiles: Made in Code*. New York: Thames & Hudson, 2012.
Copenhafer, David. "Mourning and Music in *Blue Velvet*." *Camera Obscura* 23, no. 3 (2008): 137–57.
Corber, Robert J. "Joan Crawford's Padded Shoulders: Female Masculinity in *Mildred Pierce*." *Camera Obscura* 21, no. 2 (2006): 24.
Danet, Brenda. "Pixel Patchwork: 'Quilting in Time' Online." *Textile: The Journal of Cloth and Culture* 1, no. 2 (2003): 118–43.
Danilowitz, Brenda. ed. *Anni Albers; Selected Writings on Design*. Hanover: Wesleyan University Press, 2001.
Deleuze, Gilles. *The Fold: Leibniz and the Baroque*, translated by Tom Conley. Minneapolis: University of Minnesota Press, 1993.
Deleuze, Gilles and Félix Guattari. *A Thousand Plateaus: Capitalism and Schizophrenia*, translated by Brian Massumi. Minneapolis: University of Minnesota Press, 1987.

Dirix, Emmanuelle, ed. *Unravel: Knitwear in Fashion*. Tielt: Lannoo Publishers, 2011.

Doane, Mary Ann. *The Desire to Desire: The Woman's Film of the 1940s*. Bloomington: Indiana University Press, 1987.

Doane, Mary Ann. *Femmes Fatales: Feminism, Film Theory, Psychoanalysis*. New York: Routledge, 1991.

Donkor, Godfried. "The Currency of Ntoma (Fabric)." *Textile: A Journal of Cloth and Culture* 16, no. 2 (2018): 200–13.

Dormer, Peter, ed. *The Culture of Craft: Status and Future*. Manchester: Manchester University Press, 1997.

Dormor, Catherine. "Skin: textile: film." *Textile: The Journal of Cloth and Culture* 6, no. 3 (2008): 238–53.

Dormor, Catherine. *A Philosophy of Textile: Between Practice and Theory*. London: Bloomsbury, 2020.

Doy, Gen. *Seeing and Consciousness: Women, Class, and Representation*. Oxford: Berg, 1995.

Doy, Gen. *Drapery: Classicism and Barbarism in Visual Culture*. London: I.B. Tauris, 2002.

Drazin, Charles. *Charles Drazin on Blue Velvet*. London: Bloomsbury, 1998.

DuPlessis, Robert S. *The Material Atlantic: Clothing, Commerce, and Colonization in the Atlantic World, 1650–1800*. Cambridge: Cambridge University Press, 2016.

Eicher, Joanne B., ed. *Dress and Ethnicity*. Oxford: Berg, 1995.

El Guindi, Fadwa. *Veil: Modesty, Privacy and Resistance*. Oxford: Berg, 1999.

Elsaesser, Thomas and Malte Hagener. *Film Theory: An Introduction Through the Senses*, 2nd edn. New York: Routledge, 2015.

Estad, Nan. *Ladies of Labor, Girls of Adventure: Working Women, Popular Culture, and Labor Politics at the Turn of the Twentieth Century*. New York: Columbia University Press, 1999.

Faiers, Jonathan. *Dressing Dangerously: Dysfunctional Fashion in Film*. New Haven: Yale University Press, 2013.

Fanon, Frantz. *Black Skin, White Masks*, translated by Richard Philcox. New York: Grove Press, 2008.

Felleman, Susan. *Real Objects in Unreal Situations: Modern Art in Fiction Films*. Bristol: Intellect, 2014.

Ferguson, Kevin L. "Painting in the Dark: The Ambivalence of Air in Cinema." *Camera Obscura* 26, no. 2 (2011): 32–63.

Fischer, Lucy. *Designing Women: Cinema, Art Deco, and the Female Form*. New York: Columbia University Press, 2003.

Freud, Sigmund. *Three Essays on the Theory of Sexuality*, translated by James Strachey. New York: Basic Books, 2000.

Freud, Sigmund and C. J. M Hubback. *Beyond the Pleasure Principle*. London: The International Psycho-Analytical Press, 1922.

Gaines, Jane and Charlotte Herzog, eds. *Fabrications: Costume and the Female Body*. New York: Routledge, 1990.

Gaudreault, André and Philippe Marion. *The End of Cinema?: A Medium in Crisis in the Digital Age*. New York: Columbia University Press, 2015.

Geczy, Adam. *Fashion and Orientalism: Dress, Textiles, and Culture from the 17th to the 21st Century*. London: Bloomsbury, 2013.

Gordon, Beverly. *Textiles: The Whole Story*. London: Thames and Hudson, 2011.

Gschwandtner, Sabrina. "Knitting Is . . .." In *The Textiles Reader*, edited by Jessica Hemmings, 409–18. London: Bloomsbury, 2012.

Halberstam, Jack, *Trans*: A Quick and Quirky Account of Gender Variability*. Berkeley: University of California Press, 2018.

Hamlyn, Anne. "Freud, Fabric, Fetish." In *The Textile Reader*, edited by Jessica Hemmings, 14–26. London: Bloomsbury, 2012.

Handley, Susannah. *Nylon: The Story of a Fashion Revolution*. Baltimore: The Johns Hopkins University Press, 1999.

Hansen, Karen Tranberg and D. Soyini Madison, eds. *African Dress: Fashion, Agency, Performance*. London: Bloomsbury, 2013.

Hansen, Miriam. "Pleasure, Ambivalence, Identification: Valentino and Female Spectatorship." *Cinema Journal* 25, no. 4 (1986): 6–32.

Heath, Jennifer, ed. *The Veil: Women Writers on Its History, Lore, and Politics*. Berkeley: University of California Press, 2008.

Hebdige, Dick. *Subculture: The Meaning of Style*. London: Routledge, 1979.

Hemmings, Jessica, ed. *The Textile Reader*. London: Bloomsbury, 2012.

Hemmings, Jessica, ed. *Cultural Threads: Transnational Textiles Today*. London: Bloomsbury, 2015.

Hill, Erin. *Never Done: A History of Women's Work in Media Production.* New Brunswick: Rutgers University Press, 2016.

Hoberman, J. and Edward Leffingwell, eds. *Wait for Me at the Bottom of the Pool: The Writings of Jack Smith.* New York: High Risk Books, 1997.

Hollander, Anne. *Seeing Through Clothes.* New York: Penguin Books, 1978.

Hollander, Anne. *Moving Pictures.* Cambridge, MA: Harvard University Press, 1991.

Hunt, Kevin J. "Eyes, Sight and the Senses on Film and in Fashion: Crossmodal Correspondences and Sensorial Empathy between Lars von Trier's *Dancer in the Dark* (2000) and Johan Ku's *Selma* Collection S/S (2014)." *Fashion Theory: The Journal of Dress, Body & Culture* 22, no. 1 (2018): 31–67.

Ingold, Tim. *Lines: A Brief History.* London: Routledge, 2007.

Jacobs, Steven, Susan Felleman, Vito Adriaensens, and Lisa Colpaert, eds. *Screening Statues: Sculpture and Cinema.* Edinburgh: Edinburgh University Press, 2017.

Kachurin, Pamela Jill. *Soviet Textiles: Designing the Modern Utopia.* Boston: Museum of Fine Arts Publications, 2006.

Kelley, Mike. "Cross Gender/Cross Genre." *PAJ: A Journal of Performance and Art* 22, no.1 (2000): 1–9.

Kettle, Alice and Lesley Millar, eds. *The Erotic Cloth: Seduction and Fetishism in Textiles.* London: Bloomsbury, 2018.

Knox, Kristin. *Culture to Catwalk: How World Cultures Influence Fashion.* London: A & C Black, 2011.

Koda, Harold. *Goddess: The Classical Mode.* New Haven: Yale University Press and New York: The Metropolitan Museum of Art, 2003.

Koplos, Janet and Bruce Metcalf, eds. *Makers: A History of American Studio Craft.* Chapel Hill: The University of North Carolina Press, 2010.

Kuzniar, Alice A. "Ears Looking at You: E.T.A. Hoffman's *The Sandman* and David Lynch's *Blue Velvet*." *South Atlantic Review* 54, no. 2 (1989): 7–21.

Langford, Rachael. "Black and White in Black and White Identity and Cinematography in Ousmane Sembène's *La Noire de . . . /Black Girl* (1966)." *Studies in French Cinema* 1, no. 1 (2001): 13–21.

Lant, Antonia. "The Curse of the Pharaoh, or How Cinema Contracted Egyptomania." *October* 59 (1992): 86–112.

Lant, Antonia. "Haptical Cinema." *October* 74 (1995): 45–73.
LaSalle, Mick. *Complicated Women: Sex and Power in Pre-Code Hollywood*. New York: St Martin's Press, 2000.
Livingstone, Joan and John Ploof, eds. *The Object of Labor: Art, Cloth, and Cultural Production*. Chicago: School of the Art Institute of Chicago Press, 2007.
Margulies, Ivone. *Nothing Happens: Chantal Akerman's Hyperrealist Everyday*. Durham: Duke University Press, 1996.
Marks, Laura U. *The Skin of the Film: Intercultural Cinema, Embodiment, and the Senses*. Durham: Duke University Press, 2000.
Marks, Laura U. *Touch: Sensuous Theory and Multisensory Media*. Minneapolis: University of Minnesota Press, 2002.
Martin, Florence. *Screens and Veils: Maghrebi Women's Cinema*. Bloomington: Indiana University Press, 2011.
McMahon, Laura. *Cinema and Contact: The Withdrawal of Touch in Nancy, Bresson, Duras and Denis*. New York: Routledge, 2012.
Mears, Patricia and Emma McClendon, eds. *Yves Saint Laurent + Halston: Fashioning the 70s*. New York: Fashion Institute of Technology, 2015.
Meuel, David. *Women Film Editors: Unseen Artists of American Cinema*. Jefferson: McFarland & Company, 2016.
Moon, Michael and Eve Kosofsky Sedgwick. "Divinity: A Dossier; A Performance Piece; A Little-Understood Emotion." *Discourse* 13, no. 1 (1990–1991): 12–39.
Moore, Colleen. *Silent Star*. New York: Doubleday & Co, Inc., 1968.
Mulvey, Laura. *Fetishism and Curiosity*. Bloomington: Indiana University Press, 1996.
Munich, Adrienne, ed. *Fashion in Film*. Bloomington: Indiana University Press, 2011.
Murch, Walter. *In the Blink of an Eye: A Perspective on Film Editing*, 2nd edn. Los Angeles: Silman-James Press, 2001.
Ndiaye, Pap. *Nylon and Bombs: DuPont and the March of Modern America*, translated by Elborg Forster. Baltimore: The Johns Hopkins Press, 2007.
Parvulescu, Anca. "Import/Export: Housework in an International Frame." *PMLA* 127, no. 4 (2012): 845–62.

Pastoureau, Michel. *The Devil's Cloth: A History of Stripes and Striped Fabric*, translated by Jody Gladding. New York: Columbia University Press, 1991.

Phipps, Elena. *Looking at Textiles: A Guide to Technical Terms*. Los Angeles: J. Paul Getty Museum, 2011.

Plant, Sadie. *Zeros + Ones*. London: Fourth Estate Limited, 1997.

Preciado, Paul B. *Testo Junkie: Sex, Drugs, and Biopolitics in the Pharmacopornographic Era*, translated by Bruce Benderson. New York: Feminist Press, 2013.

Rabine, Leslie W. *The Global Circulation of African Fashion*. Oxford: Berg, 2002.

Repinecz, Jonathon. "'This is Not a Pipe'?: Reflexivity, Fictionality, and Diologism in Sembène's Films." *Journal of African Cinemas* 8, no. 2 (2016): 181–97.

Rivers, Victoria Z. *The Shining Cloth: Dress and Adornment that Glitter*. New York: Thames & Hudson, 1999.

Roach, Joseph. *It*. Ann Arbor: The University of Michigan Press, 2007.

Rocamora, Agnès and Anneke Smelik, eds. *Thinking Through Fashion: A Guide to Key Theorists*. London: I.B. Tauris, 2015.

Rosen, Philip, ed. *Narrative, Apparatus, Ideology: A Film Theory Reader*. New York: Columbia University Press, 1986.

Ross, Doran H. *Wrapped in Pride: Ghanaian Kente and African American Identity*. Los Angeles: University of California Los Angleles Fowler Museum of Cultural History, 1998.

Rowe, Carel. *The Baudelairean Cinema: A Trend Within the American Avant-Garde*. Ann Arbor: University of Michigan Press, 1982.

Said, Edward W. *Orientalism*. New York: Random House, 1979.

Scanlan, Jennifer. "Crafting With and Against the Grid." *The Journal of Modern Craft* 8, no. 2 (2015): 215–24.

Schoeser, Mary. *World Textiles: A Concise History*. London: Thames & Hudson, 2003.

Schor, Naomi. *Reading in Detail: Aesthetics and the Feminine*. New York: Routledge, 2007.

Schwartz, Hillel. *The Culture of the Copy: Striking Likenesses, Unreasonable Facsimiles*. New York: Zone Books, 1996.

Serano, Julia. *Whipping Girl: A Transexual Woman on Sexism and the Scapegoating of Femininity*. Berkeley: Seal Press, 2016.
Shaviro, Steven. *The Cinematic Body*. Minneapolis: University of Minnesota Press, 1993.
Shulman, Alexandra. *Clothes . . . And Other Things that Matter*. London: Cassell, 2020.
Silver, Alain and James Ursini, eds. *Film Noir Reader*. New York: Limelight, 1996.
Smith, T'ai. *Bauhaus Weaving Theory: From Feminine Craft to Mode of Design*. Minneapolis: University of Minnesota Press, 2014.
Smulyan, Susan. *Popular Ideologies: Mass Culture at Mid-Century*. Philadelphia: University of Pennsylvania Press, 2007.
Sobchack, Vivian. *Carnal Thoughts: Embodiment and Moving Image Culture*. Berkeley: University of California Press, 2004.
Solnit, Rebecca. *River of Shadows: Eadweard Muybridge and the Technological Wild West*. New York: Penguin Books, 2003.
Sowinska, Alicja. "Dialectic of the Banana Skirt: The Ambiguities of Josephine Baker's Self-Representation." *Michigan Feminist Studies* 19 (2005–2006): 51–72.
Steele, Valerie. *Fetish: Fashion, Sex & Power*. Oxford: Oxford University Press, 1997.
Steele, Valerie. *The Corset: A Cultural History*. New Haven: Yale University Press, 2001.
Steinbock, Eliza. *Shimmering Images: Trans Cinema, Embodiment, and the Aesthetics of Change*. Durham: Duke University Press, 2019.
Stewart, Jude. *Patternalia: An Unconventional History of Polka Dots, Stripes, Plaid, Camouflage, & Other Graphic Patterns*. London: Bloomsbury, 2015.
Stewart, Susan. *On Longing*. Durham: Duke University Press, 1993.
Stoller, Robert. *Observing the Erotic Imagination*. New Haven: Yale University Press, 1985.
Strauven, Wanda. "Early Cinema's Touch(able) Screens: From Uncle Josh to Ali Barbouyou." *European Journal of Media Studies* 1, no. 2 (2012): 155–76.
Street, Sarah. *Costume and Cinema: Dress Codes in Popular Film*. London: Wallflower, 2001.

Sylvanus, Nina. *Patterns in Circulation: Cloth, Gender, and Materiality in West Africa*. Chicago: The University of Chicago Press, 2016.

Taylor, Lou. "De-coding the Hierarchy of Fashion Textiles." In *The Textiles Reader*, edited by Jessica Hemmings, 419–29. London: Bloomsbury, 2012.

Tinkcom, Matthew. *Working Like a Homosexual: Camp, Capital, Cinema*. Durham: Duke University Press, 2002.

Tortora, Phyllis G. *Dress, Fashion, and Technology: From Prehistory to Present*. London: Bloomsbury, 2015.

Trotter, David. "Lynne Ramsay's *Ratcatcher*: Towards a Theory of Haptic Narrative." *Paragraph* 21, no. 2 (July 2008): 138–58.

Truffaut, François. *The Films in My Life*. Boston: Da Capo Press, 1994.

Uhlirova, Marketa, ed. *Birds of Paradise: Costume as Cinematic Spectacle*. London: Koenig Books, 2013.

Vertov, Dziga. *Kino-Eye: The Writings of Dziga Vertov*. Berkeley: University of California Press, 1985.

Walton, Saige. *Cinema's Baroque Flesh: Film, Phenomenology and the Art of Entanglement*. Amsterdam: Amsterdam University Press, 2016.

Walton, Saige and Nadine Boljkovac. "Introduction: Materialising Absence." *Screening the Past* 43 (2018): 1–6.

Whitehead, Jean. *Creating Interior Atmosphere: Mise-en-scène and Interior Design*. London: Bloomsbury, 2017.

Wilson, Cintra. *Fear and Clothing: Unbuckling American Style*. New York: W.W. Norton, 2015.

Wilson, Elizabeth. *Adorned in Dreams: Fashion and Modernity*. London: I.B. Tauris, 2003.

Worth, Rachel. *Fashion and Class*. London: Bloomsbury, 2020.

Yeshiva University Museum. *A Perfect Fit: The Garment Industry and American Jewry 1860–1960*. New York: Yeshiva University Museum, 2005.

Filmography

A Fool There Was (dir. Frank Powell, 1915), Fox Film Corporation.
Black Girl (dir. Ousmane Sembène, 1966), Doomireew Films.
Black Narcissus (dir. Michael Powell and Emeric Pressburger, 1947), ITV Global Entertainment Ltd.
Black Panther (2018, dir. Ryan Coogler), Marvel.
Blue Velvet (dir. David Lynch, 1986), De Laurentiis Entertainment Group, Inc.
Clotheslines (dir. Roberta Cantow, 1981), Roberta Cantow.
Coming to America (dir. John Landis, 1988), Paramount.
Dancing Lady (dir. Robert Z. Leonard, 1933), Turner Entertainment Co.
Flying Down to Rio (dir. Thornton Freeland, 1933), Warner.
Gabbeh (dir. Mohsen Makhmalbaf, 1996), MK2 Productions.
In the Mood for Love (dir. Wong Kar-wai, 2000), October Films, Inc.
It Happened One Night (dir. Frank Capra, 1934), Columbia Pictures Industries, Inc.
Jeanne Dielman 23, quai du commerce, 1080 Bruxelles (dir. Chantal Akerman, 1975), Paradise Films.
La Belle et la Bête (dir. Jean Cocteau, 1946), Comité Cocteau.
Mahogany (dir. Berry Gordy, 1975), Paramount Pictures.
Man with a Movie Camera (dir. Dziga Vertov, 1929), British Film Institute.
Metropolis (dir. Fritz Lang, 1927), UFA.
Mildred Pierce (dir. Michael Curtiz, 1945), Warner Bros.
Pandora's Box (dir. G.W. Pabst, 1929), Praesens Film AG.
Pickpocket (dir. Robert Bresson, 1959), Agnès Delahaie Preoductions Cinématographie.
Polyester (dir. John Waters, 1981), New Line Cinema Corporation.
Posthaste Perennial Pattern (dir. Jodie Mack, 2010), Jodie Mack.
Puce Moment (dir. Kenneth Anger, 1949), Fantoma Films.

Querelle (dir. Rainer Werner Fassbinder, 1982), Gaumont.
Rebecca (dir. Alfred Hitchcock, 1940), ABC, Inc.
Ritual in Transfigured Time (dir. Maya Deren, 1945–6), Mystic Fire Video.
Roberta (dir. William Seiter, 1935), RKO Pictures, Inc.
Saturday Night Fever (dir. John Badham, 1977), Paramount Pictures.
Shanghai Express (dir. Josef von Sternberg, 1932), Paramount Pictures.
Sherlock, Jr. (dir. Buster Keaton, 1924), Joseph M. Schenck Productions.
Singin' in the Rain (dir. Stanley Donen, 1952), Warner Bros.
Spellbound (dir. Alfred Hitchcock, 1945), ABC, Inc.
The Assassin (dir. Hou Hsiao-Hsien, 2015), Spotfilms Ltd.
The Cheat (dir. Cecil B. DeMille, 1915), A Paramount Picture.
The Cobweb (1955, dir. Vincente Minnelli), Metro-Goldwyn-Mayer.
The Man in the White Suit (dir. Alexander Mackendrick, 1951), Studio Canal Films Ltd.
The Matrix (dir. The Wachowski Brothers, 1999), Warner Bros.
The Sheik (dir. George Melford, 1921), Paramount Pictures.
The Skin I Live In (dir. Pedro Almodóvar, 2011), El Deseo.
The Stepford Wives (dir. Bryan Forbes, 1975), Palomar Pictures.
Top Hat (dir. Mark Sandrich, 1935), RKO Pictures, Inc.
Under the Skin (dir. Jonathan Glazer, 2013), British Film Institute.
Who are You, Polly Maggoo? (dir. William Klein, 1966), Delpire.

Index

Adamson, Glenn   9–10
Akerman, Chantal   61–3
Albers, Anni   9, 20
Allmer, Açalya   127
Anger, Kenneth   51, 80, 129–30, 146
Art Deco   19, 27–8, 31, 35, 40
artifice   50–3, 58, 80–1, 134
Ash, Juliet   68–9
Assassin, The (2015)   162
Auther, Elissa   59, 134, 152–3

Bachelard, Gaston   116
Baker, Josephine   146
Barker, Jennifer M.   92, 104
Barnett, Pennina   93, 124–5, 167–8
Baroque art   106, 116, 124–5
Barthes, Roland   15, 51–2, 161
Benjamin, Walter   13, 48, 96
Black Girl (1966)   70–5
Black Narcissus (1947)   115–20, 123
Blue Velvet (1986)   95–104
Bresson, Robert   93
Brinkema, Eugenie   12, 161
Bruno, Giuliana   46, 106, 136–7
Bruzzi, Stella   83

celluloid   46–7
Cheat, The (1918)   162
cinematography   20–1, 50, 63, 67–8, 83, 94, 112, 115
Clark, Judith   140
class separation   23, 45–9, 63, 81–2, 125–6
Cocteau, Jean   124–5
Copenhafer, David   104

Corber, Robert J.   87
craft   59–60, 134, 136
criminality   78, 88, 93–5, 99, 101
curtaining   101–2, 114, 123–4, 126–30

dance   21–2, 25–6, 112–13, 129, 132
Dancing Lady (1933)   33–4
Deleuze, Gilles   93, 106, 116
Deren, Maya   131–4
digital media   135–6
Doane, Mary Ann   146, 165
domestic labor   7, 13, 45–6, 58–63, 73–5, 83, 126
Donen, Stanley   113
Dormor, Catherine   123, 147
Doy, Gen   108, 129, 144
draping   21, 92, 108, 111
Drazin, Charles   98
DuPont Corporation   44, 46

Elsaesser, Thomas   127, 141–2
Evans, Caroline   69
experimental film   8–9, 129

Fanon, Frantz   157
Fassbinder, Rainer Werner   79–80
Fellini, Frederico   56
femininity   51, 53, 55–7, 63, 87
femme fatale   38–9, 75, 77–8, 83–4
Ferguson, Kevin L.   115
fetish   95–7, 99–100
film editing   2, 4–5, 7, 27, 34–5, 103–4, 112, 121, 124, 131, 134
Fischer, Lucy   23, 28, 145–6

A Fool There Was (1915)   67, 75–8
frayage   15, 117, 123
Freud, Sigmund   96, 99
fur   95–6

Gaines, Jane M.   145
Gaultier, Jean-Paul   79
Geczy, Adam   76
Genet, Jean   79
ghosts   119–22, 130
Gilligan, Sarah   106
Gordon, Beverly   69–70
Gschwandtner, Sabrina   xi, 14

Hagener, Malte   127, 141–2
Halberstam, Jack   52
Hamlyn, Anne   99–100, 159
Handley, Susannah   45
Hansen, Karen Tranberg   73
Hayes Code   22, 31–2, 114
Hebdige, Dick   78–9
Herzog, Charlotte   144
Hindson, Catherine   112
Hitchcock, Alfred   120, 165
Hollander, Anne   140–1

imprisonment   65–9, 81–2, 84–7
In the Mood for Love (2000)   105–7
interior design   7, 63, 86–7, 106–7, 165
intimacy   102, 107–8, 132–3
It Happened One Night (1934)   22, 107–8

Jeanne Dielman, 23, quai du commerce, 1080 Bruxelles (1976)   61

Kar-Wai, Wong   105
Kelleher, Katy   50
Kelley, Mike   53
kente cloth   154–5
Koda, Harold   144

Koestenbaum, Wayne   79
Kuzniar, Alice   100

La Belle et la Bête (1946)   124–7
Lang, Fritz   37
Langford, Rachael   70
LaSalle, Mick   31–2, 76
Leslie, Esther   35, 47, 140

McMahon, Laura   94
Mack, Jodie   133–4
Mahogany (1975)   163
Man in the White Suit, The (1951)   45
Man with a Movie Camera (1929)   1–2, 134
Margulies, Ivone   62–3
Marks, Laura U.   11, 95, 105
mass production   3, 41, 44–5, 47–8, 134
Matrix, The (1999)   150–1
memory   92, 94, 96, 105, 123, 130
Metropolis (1927)   37–9
Meuel, David   140
Michelson, Annette   139
Mildred Pierce (1945)   82–8
Miodownik, Mark   47
mise-en-scène   7–8, 23, 37, 67, 79–80, 87, 99–100, 106, 111, 125, 140
Montross, Sarah   95
Morris, Kathleen   9
Mulvey, Laura   145
Murch, Walter   103–4
museums   91
Muybridge, Eadweard   112

narrative   8, 23, 80
natural fibers   46, 52
Ndiaye, Pap   44
New Woman, The   21, 28, 31
Ngai, Sianne   12, 55
Nights of Cabiria (1957)   56

nonverbal communication 69–70, 105, 114, 132
nylon 44

Osterweil, Ara 38

Pabst, G.W. 29–31
Padovani, Clio 102
Pandora's Box (1929) 29–32
Parker, Rozsika 59
Parvulescu, Anca 61
Pastoureau, Michel 66
Peau d'âne (1970) x
Phipps, Elena 19
Pickpocket (1959) 93–5
Plant, Sadie 136–7, 154
plastic 51–2, 58
political struggle
    feminist 58, 65
    LGBTQIA+ 53, 59, 65, 78–80
    postcolonial 65, 70–4, 115
Polyester (1981) 54–8
Posthaste Perennial Pattern (2010) 133–4
Preciado, Paul B. 58
privacy 86, 105, 107
Puce Moment (1949) 129–30
Purple Rose of Cairo, The (1985) 160

Querelle (1982) 79–82

Rabine, Leslie W. 74
racism 28–9, 53, 71–4, 87
Rebecca (1940) 120–2
Rideal, Liz 106, 113
Ritual in Transfigured Time (1946) 131–3
Rivers, Victoria 37
Roberta (1935) 28–9

satin 19–21, 25–9, 37
Saturday Night Fever (1977) 48–51
scent 54, 116

Schaag, Katie 150
Schor, Naomi 10, 12–13
scissors 2, 103–4
Sembène, Ousmane 70–1
Seven-Year Itch, The (1955) 164
sexuality 13, 51, 76–8, 80
Shanghai Express (1932) 162
Sheik, The (1921) 163–4
Sherlock Jr. (1924) 160
Shulman, Alexandra 97
silent film 111, 129–30
Singin' in the Rain (1952) 113
Sirk, Douglas 54, 80
Skin I Live In, The (2011) 151
Smith, Jack 166
Smith, T'ai 9
Smulyan, Susan 46
Sobchack, Vivian 11
Solnit, Rebecca 3, 111–12
sound 54, 100–4
Steele, Valerie 144
Steinbock, Eliza 150
Stepford Wives, The (1975) 60–1
Stoller, Robert 99
stripes 65–70, 78, 80–2
suspense 89, 114, 120–1, 132

tactility 7, 11, 43, 63, 93, 101
    prohibition against touch 66, 88, 91–2, 105–7
tapestry 8
Taylor, Lou 47
technology 3, 38, 47, 67, 69, 111–12, 133–5
theatrical stage 79–80, 91, 123–4, 126–7, 135
Tinkcom, Matthew 129
Toepfer, Karl 38
Top Hat (1935) 25–7
Tortora, Phyllis G. 148
transgender identity 52, 57
Truffaut, François 25, 145

Under the Skin (2013) 38–40

velvet   95–105
Vertov, Dziga   1–2, 5, 134

Walton, Saige   165
Waters, John   53–4, 60

What Happened on Twenty-Third Street, New York City (1901)   164
Whittaker, Paul   102
wind   114–19, 127–8
Worth, Rachel   44

www.ingramcontent.com/pod-product-compliance
Lightning Source LLC
Chambersburg PA
CBHW052120300426
44116CB00010B/1739